Ayodhya
Ram Mandir

Swadesh Singh is an author, teacher and activist. Educated at Jawaharlal Nehru University and Indian Institute of Mass Communication, New Delhi, his professional experience spans more than 15 years during which he has worked with reputed media organizations in the national capital. He currently teaches Political Science in Delhi University. He has four books to his credit and regularly writes for newspapers, online platforms and academic journals.

'After being denied justice for centuries, the Ram Janmabhoomi temple once again stands tall. As the king of Ayodhya returns to his seat, we must also bring him back to our discourse. This beautiful book marks the beginning of the return of Lord Ram to Ayodhya.'

—**Anand Ranganathan**, Scientist and Author

'The re-making of Ram mandir is a major milestone in the civilizational march of Bharat. This book beautifully chronicles the series of events that have led to this historic moment. A timely and much-needed book.'

—**Uday Mahurkar**, Author and Senior Journalist

'The inauguration of a grand Rama Temple in Ayodhya by Prime Minister Narendra Modi in January 2024 is a landmark moment in India's civilizational journey. Lord Rama's exile of over five centuries, comes to an end, and with it, the spiritual-cultural heritage of India prepares to take centre stage. Dr Swadesh Singh's book is a timely chronicle of that journey.'

—**Meenakshi Jain**, Historian and Author

Ayodhya
Ram Mandir
Bharat's Quest for Ram-Rajya

Swadesh Singh

RUPA

Published by
Rupa Publications India Pvt Ltd 2024
7/16, Ansari Road, Daryaganj
New Delhi 110002

Sales centres:
Bengaluru Chennai
Hyderabad Jaipur Kathmandu
Kolkata Mumbai Prayagraj

P-ISBN: 978-93-5702-864-6
E-ISBN: 978-93-5702-713-7

First impression 2024

10 9 8 7 6 5 4 3 2 1

The moral right of the author has been asserted.

Printed in India

Dedicated to
Shri Ashok Singhal ji and a million others who devoted
and sacrificed their lives for the construction of the Ram
Janmabhoomi Temple in Ayodhya

CONTENTS

INTRODUCTION

Await the Arrival

Hari Anant, Hari Katha Ananta,
Kahahi Sunahi Bahuvidhi Sab Santa.[1]

[Lord Shri Ram is limitless, as are his stories,
Many saints relate Lord Ram's glory in many
different ways.]

The secret to human survival lies in its faith, its belief in the very existence and power of a saviour. Every era searches for this one ideal figure, someone who can be loved and followed by the masses. It is a rare occurrence in any epoch to stumble upon such a figure; rarer are those figures that remain relevant across ages. Through the journey of one of the oldest civilizations in documented history, followers of Hinduism have relied upon one such ideal to help them navigate the grey areas of human morality. Leading by example, Lord Ram has transcended time and space as the ideal man—the *Maryada Purushottam* (the most dignified man). It is thus no surprise that since time immemorial, he has been accorded the status of God.

Ram is a devoted son, a brave warrior and, above all, an ideal king whose reign stands as a symbol for impeccable governance, and his kingdom represents a utopian state, the *Ram-Rajya*. The lettered read about it in the Ramayana, the unlettered hear of it through word of mouth. Regardless, all worship Lord Ram.

Valmiki's Ramayana gave us our idol whose journey became an integral lesson for the Hindu way of life. His story resonated with learned men and women. It crossed the seven seas, along with worshippers who took a little of him, Sita and Ayodhya with them wherever they went.

Today, Ram's followers—at home in India to Suriname on the other side of the globe—pay salutations to the divine power. The cultures and religious beliefs of several countries resonate with the preachings of Ramayana and that of Lord Ram. This holds especially true for the South Asian countries of India, Nepal and Sri Lanka, which are closely associated with the divine story, each finding mention in the main epic as either the place of origin for various characters or as the setting of various scenes.

Ram is an inalienable part of the living civilizational memory of South Asia and Southeast Asia. The ideals of Ram are celebrated and worshipped in countries like Indonesia, Mauritius and Thailand, placing him at the core of our lives and cultural memory. For instance, the ruling royal family of Thailand (Chakri dynasty) has adopted 'Rama' as the monarchy's nomenclature—the current king is known to his people and the world as King Rama X.

It is not only the legends of Lord Ram but the entire story of Ramayana that has travelled across the globe. The renditions of Ramcharitmanas are also a part of the daily life of many in Mauritius and Caribbean countries. Courtesy of the Hindu influence over Southeast Asia, many countries in the region have their own versions of the legend.

Reamker is the version of the Ramayana that is popular in Cambodia and is believed to have arrived in Cambodia around the seventh century. The Kakawin Ramayana is the Indonesian version written in old Javanese language, which is believed to have come to Indonesia around the eighth or ninth century. It played a role in reviving Hinduism during a period when Buddhism held strong influence in Sumatra, West Java and Central Java, utilizing shadow puppetry. The Kakawin Ramayana is believed to have been written during the Medang Kingdom (732–1006 CE) in Central Java.[2]

Phra Lak Phra Lam is the version of Ramayana that is prevalent in Laos and is also their national epic. The title of the retelling is named after the two brothers, Phra Lak (Lakshman) and Phra Lam (Ram). In Laos, where Theravada Buddhism is prominent, this rendition is viewed as a Jataka story—an account of the earlier lives of Buddha. The story takes place along the Mekong River. Phra Ram is regarded as the past manifestation of Gautama Buddha, symbolizing moral leadership and unwavering commitment to his dharma, while Hapmanasouane, the Lao counterpart to Ravan, is seen as the former incarnation of Mara, the demon who sought to obstruct the Buddha on his path to enlightenment.[3]

The Ramayana in Malaysia is used more for entertainment and social education rather than for spiritual or religious purposes. The Hikayat Seri Rama, a Malay adaptation of the Ramayana, serves as a platform to highlight the virtues of righteousness, love, loyalty and selfless devotion.

Drawing inspiration from the Indian Sanskrit Ramayana and incorporating local traditions and beliefs, it weaves a rich narrative that resonates with many, showcasing a harmonious blend of cultural elements.[4]

The legend crossed seven seas to reach the other side of the world. The Ramayana tradition along with the ideals of Ram was carried to the Caribbean countries by indentured labourers. Since the epic was introduced there, it has occupied an unchallenged position as a *Dharmashastra* (holy writ) in all facets of Hindu life. Among the Caribbean countries, the Ramayana tradition is majorly prevalent in Trinidad and Tobago, Suriname and Guyana where a substantial portion of the indentured labourers were from Uttar Pradesh (UP) and Bihar. The Ramayana has also exercised a significant influence on the culture of Trinidad and Tobago. V.S. Naipaul, perhaps the most celebrated product of the Trinidad Hindu community, described the Ramayana as something that lived among them. Ramlila—the dramatic folk re-enactment of the Ramayana—is attended by the Hindus in Trinidad in thousands.[5] This celebration of Ramlila was eloquently conveyed by the late poet and playwright Derek Walcott during his 1992 Nobel Prize for Literature acceptance speech, where he stated: 'Here in Trinidad I discovered that one of the greatest epics of the world was seasonally performed, not with that desperate resignation of preserving a culture, but with an openness of belief that was as steady as the wind bending the cane lances of the Caroni plain.'[6]

The impact and influence of Ram is not limited to the moral or cultural domain. It reaches far beyond the defined realms of religion and offers to the society a model of polity and justice that is supreme. In Hindu terminology, this idea, derived from the lessons of Ram's governance, is called Ram-Rajya.

Ram-Rajya is considered as an ideal form of governance, something that Gandhi ji envisioned as an ideal state for free India. Thus, the reign of Lord Ram in the kingdom of Kosala is said to be marked by an era of righteousness, prosperity, progress and peace.[7] As per the concept, the king is expected to embrace austerity, generosity, kindness, justice, a focus on welfare and the ability to care for and plan for the well-being of all his subjects.[8]

Ayodhya, the capital of the kingdom of Kosala, currently situated in the state of UP, is central to the narrative of Lord Ram. Being his birthplace, it is considered sacred by his worshippers, as are the many temples built in and around Ayodhya. Also, in the vicinity of Ayodhya are several holy sites tied to the life and lore of Shri Ram, such as Shri Ram Janmabhoomi, Sita Ki Rasoi (kitchen of Sita), Hanumangarhi, Sugreev Kila, Bharat Kund, Shrigverpur, Bharadwaj Ashram, Panchwati and many others. All these places are intrinsically linked to the culture and civilization of India and are considered sacred.

Many of these places were plundered and destroyed during the medieval times. A mosque was built in place of Shri Ram Janmabhoomi Temple (the holy birth site). There are not just one, but several attacks on Ayodhya and other sites during this period. However, the local community rebuilt the temple time and again.[9] During the British Raj, in the late nineteenth century, a case was filed to reclaim the Ram Janmabhoomi Temple. Without any conclusive answers, the conflict led on and, in the late twentieth century, a mass movement took shape in the form of the Ram Janmabhoomi

Movement, also commonly called as the Ram Temple or Ram Mandir Movement, which heralded a new debate at the national level. There have been many other agitations and movements on different issues which were crushed or weakened but there was continuity in the struggle for the Ram temple in Ayodhya. The reason for this continuity lies in the fact that the first line of leadership in the Ram Temple Movement came from the sadhu community who travelled extensively across the country, interacting with the people and spreading the message of hope, unity and the need to strive for Ram Lalla's (the infant form of Ram) right to his land.

A long and protracted legal, social, political and cultural battle culminated on 9 November 2019. On this day, the Supreme Court of India declared its verdict in favour of the temple on the basis of evidences, including historical testimonies presented by the Archaeological Survey of India (ASI). Immediately after the verdict, a trust was formed and was given the responsibility to build the Ram Janmabhoomi Temple in Ayodhya. The construction process started in full swing in 2021 giving an impetus to the overall development of the Ayodhya city. The temple is set to be open to public in January 2024 and a grand ceremony is expected to take place on 22 January 2024.

Construction of Shri Ram Janmabhoomi Temple in Ayodhya is the outcome of a 500-year-long struggle. While several scholarly works have been written about this protracted struggle, this book attempts to provide a brief account of the new Shri Ram Janmabhoomi Temple in Ayodhya, as well as the beliefs, practices and legends associated with it.

Ram and Ramayana are inseparable from the Indian culture and ethos. The book combines history, legality and social aspects of the Ram Janmabhoomi to bring to the readers a view of the conflict, the final verdict and the victory of Indian secularism. Chapter one locates the story of Ayodhya across legends and history. This journey begins with the Ikshvaku dynasty and visits different milestones of Mauryan, Gupta and Islamic periods up to the British era. Chapter two goes over the court cases that were fought to claim the Ram temple land. The first case was filed in 1822. Consecutively, post Independence, after a Ram Lalla idol was found in the disputed structure, the worship of Ram Lalla was started again on the said land.[10] In the 1980s, along with the court cases, a mass mobilization took place in the form of the Ram Temple Movement to build a grand temple in Ayodhya. This movement would change the socio-political landscape of the country in later years. Chapter three focuses on the court and the people, documenting their participation, and the verdict and its reception. Finally, in 2019, the Supreme Court of India delivered its verdict in favour of Ram Lalla and the injustice meted out for 500 years moved towards gaining closure.

In chapter four, our focus turns to the recent construction of the Ram Temple in Ayodhya. This chapter gives a bird's eye view of the endeavours for the construction of the Ram Temple, including the design, the land and the idols, among other things. Lastly, chapter five looks at the grand transformation unfolding in Ayodhya with the construction of the Ram Temple and the impact that it hopes to have on the way India views the intersection of secularism and development. This chapter covers all the burgeoning work being undertaken in Ayodhya, propelling the city on to the international tourist map.

As the nation waits for their God to reside in His rightful place, the completion of the Ram Temple in Ayodhya is a ray of hope. Through the holes in the political fabric of India and the ups and downs of Hindu–Muslim relations, the temple makes way for peace, acceptance, tolerance and unity for all Indians—followers of the faith and otherwise. The Ram Temple Movement's history serves as evidence that, in India, any controversial issue can be resolved through a democratic process, and that the quest for Ram-Rajya will go on.

1

ALONG THE SARAYU,
LIES THE INVINCIBLE

Ayodhya Mathura Maya Kasi Kanchi Avantika
Puri Dvaravati chaiva saptaita moksadayikah.

[The seven cities of Ayodhya, Mathura, Maya (Mayapura),
Kanci, Avantika (Jagannatha Puri), Kasi and Dvaravati
(Dvaraka) confer salvation.[1]]

There is a river—Ghaghara—that takes a long route;
its waters cascade from the Himalayan highlands to
the plains. Known by several names, she flows through
many cities, each of which have accepted the river's varied
nomenclature. Once it enters the plains of UP, the mighty
Ghaghara adapts to the unison of being called Sarayu.
Situated on the banks of this river, is one of the holiest *tirtha*s
(sacred places) in the Hindu mythology—Ayodhya.

Ayodhya has been a sacred city for the Hindus since
time immemorial. The place has survived the vicissitudes

of history and, in successive historical eras, has continued to retain its revered position in the Hindu way of life. The current chapter examines the history of Ayodhya—the first step to understanding how the place continue to hold a prominent spiritual position in Hinduism. The chapter traces the history of Ayodhya, from antiquity to the modern era when Ayodhya came under the influence of the British rule.

Broadly, Hindu mythology divides human history into four epochs or *yuga*s, namely the Sat Yuga, Treta Yuga, Dvapara Yuga and Kali Yuga. Each of the yuga is said to be marked by a gradual degradation of human values and morality and a rise in materialism. The Sat Yuga is believed to be a period of truth, purity and spiritual enlightenment, while the Treta Yuga is regarded as the age of rituals and sacrifices, marking a shift from inner spirituality. The word 'treta' signifies 'collection of three'—in this case, the fifth, sixth and seventh avatars of Vishnu in the form of Vaman, Parasuram and Ram respectively.[2] The events of the second yuga have found their mention in the first poem in classical Sanskrit literature—Valmiki's Ramayana, also called as Adikavya. The epic is the narration of Lord Ram's life, along with the journey of his family and his kingdom.

The sacred city of Ayodhya not only finds mention; it is prominently referred to in ancient and mythological literature, unrestricted by language, region or medium of exchange. The centrality of the riverbank city is directly related to it being the birthplace and home of the revered Hindu deity Lord Ram. The city serves as the stage where his life unfolds along with his values and morals, which inevitably throw light on the general, social, religious and moral aspects of life in that epoch of Hindu mythology and history.

OLDER THAN ANCIENT

As per the Mahabharata, Ayodhya was known as Punyalaksana, meaning 'that which is endowed with auspicious signs'. While the Vishnu Purana refers to the city as Kosalanagara, which means 'the city of Kosala', Vividhatirthakalpa, a fourteenth century Jain text, calls the riverbank city by various names—Saketa, Ikshavakubhumi, Ramapuri and Kosala.[3] But of all the documented names, the city has most commonly come to be recognized and known as Ayodhya, the invincible land of Lord Ram. Finding its etymological roots in the Sanskrit word '*yudh*' or 'war', Ayodhya loosely translates into the city that is invincible and unconquerable.[4]

As per the Brahmanda Purana, being regarded as the birthplace of one of the most revered Hindu gods and the prosperous capital of kingdom of Kosala, Ayodhya is among the foremost sacred cities of India, along with Mathura, Kashi, Kanchi, Haridwar, Avantika and Dwarka. Similarly, the Skanda Purana too adds to the mythological superiority of the city by stating that Ayodhya is an embodiment of Brahma, Vishnu and Rudra.[5]

According to ancient Indian literature, Ayodhya was the capital of Ikshavaku dynasty to which Lord Ram belonged. According to the Ramayana, Vaivatsa Manu, son of Vivasvan (the Sun), founded the city of Ayodhya.[6] Manu had ten children, of whom Ikshvaku, the eldest, became the next ruler of the Kosala kingdom. The Valmiki Ramayana states, 'In the country called Kosala was the famous capital city of Ayodhya built by the lord of men, Manu. With well-laid-out thoroughfares, the beautiful and prosperous city of Ayodhya extended for twelve yojanas in length and three yojanas in breadth'.[7]

According to the Puranas, there had been 64 kings of the Kosala kingdom before Ram.[8] Dashrath was the father of Lord Ram. His birth name was Nemi but he acquired the name Dashrath as he could move his chariot in all ten directions. His three main throne queens were Kausalya, Kekayi and Sumitra; and from these unions were born Ram, Lakshman, Bharat and Shatrughan. According to the Valmiki Ramayana, Lord Ram was born in the eighty-first generation of the Ikshvaku dynasty or the Suryavansh, the solar dynasty. The line of kings from the beginning till the reign of Lord Ram, according to the Valmiki Ramayana, is: Manu, Ikshvaku, Kukshi, Vikukshi, Bana, Anaranya, Prithu, Trisanku, Dhundhumara, Yuvnasva, Mandhata, Susandhi, Dhruvasandhi, Bharata, Asita, Sagara, Asmanjas, Ansuman, Dileepa, Bhageeratha, Kukustha, Raghu, Privaddh, Shankhan, Sudarshan, Agnivarna, Shighragra, Maru, Prashushuk, Ambrish, Nuhush, Yayati, Nabhaag, Aj, Dashrath, Ram.[9]

For many centuries, the descendants of Lord Ram continued their reign in Ayodhya before it was deserted. The accounted history of Ayodhya finds some gap between the end of the Ikshavaku dynasty and its re-emergence under the Mauryan empire (322–185 BCE).

AYODHYA, SAKETA, AWADH

After several centuries, Kosala was conquered by the kings of Magadha and merged into their newly rising empire, which grew stronger during the reign of the Nandas. There is barely any reference to Ayodhya or Kosala during the

Nanda period and later the Mauryan period. Towards the end of the Mauryan rule, however, we get a vivid glimpse of Kosala in the Sanskrit work Yuga Purana, in a section of the Gargi Samhita. This work mentions an invasion of the Greeks (*yavana* or foreigners) who took possession of Pataliputra after having attacked Saketa, Panchala and Mathura. In the Mahabhashya of Patanjali, Saketa is mentioned in several places and a significant remark is made, 'Yavanas seized Saketa', thus indicating that Ayodhya was a fortified city during that time.[10]

The decline of the Mauryan empire was marked by the emergence of another powerful dynasty, the Sunga dynasty (185 BCE). Pushyamitra Sunga, who overthrew the last Mauryan king Brihadratha, annexed Ayodhya in his empire. He performed two great horse sacrifices (Ashvamedha Yajnas) on the tradition of the great Ikshvaku kings. During his rule (187–151 BCE), Ayodhya was the cultural capital of Magadha.[11] The city lay within Sunga dominion for about sixty years beginning 187 BCE, ever since Pushyamitra Sunga's reign started. In the post-Sunga period, Dhanadeva of the Deva dynasty was an important king. In fact, we know of Pushyamitra Sunga performing horse sacrifices through an inscription from Dhanadeva's time.[12]

During the reign of Kanishka, the holy city came under the rule of the Kushana empire (127–150 CE). Evidence of Kushana rule over Ayodhya can be inferred from several archaeological evidences in the form of coins and sculptures. Ayodhya emerged as a great cultural centre during the Kushana period. The great poet Asvaghosha, author of the Mahayana-shraddhotpada-shastra (The Awakening of Faith in the Mahayana) and the Buddhacarita (The Life of Buddha), was a native of the city and had migrated to Pataliputra.

This makes it clear that apart from its association with Hinduism, Ayodhya also became associated with Buddhism and Jainism. Traditional Buddhist literature refers to Ayodhya as Saketa. The association of Buddha with this city is also well known. Buddhist sources mention that Buddha lived in the garden of Saketa called Anjanavana. It was here that he had delivered his sermon in which he had expounded the concepts of joy and grief called the Saketasutta.[13]

Buddhist texts further mention that a number of other sages lived in the city of Saketa and held discussions with Lord Buddha. Sources also mention that Kakajala, a businessman of this place, became the follower of Buddha and also donated his garden called Kalakarma to Buddha. Jivaka, the famous physician of Taxila had also visited Saketa on his way to Sravasti.[14]

The Jataka stories associated with Buddha also indicate the history of Ayodhya. The *atitavathhu* (the narrative of the past) part of the Jatakas throws light on the early history of Ayodhya and its rulers. For example, the Dasarathajataka throws light on the historicity of Ram, the son of Dashrath.[15] Gautama Buddha's Phena Sutta (The Foam) is said to have been composed in Ayodhya. The Buddhist scripture Samyutta Nikaya speaks of the Buddha dwelling in Ayojjha. The sacred city's association with Buddhism can also be inferred from the account of the foreign travellers and historians who contend that Ayojjha represents the Sanskrit Ayodhya of the Ramayana and the A-yu-te of Hiuen Tsiang.[16]

Fa-Hien, a Chinese traveller who visited India around 400 CE called Ayodhya as Sha Chi. Describing the social, economic and cultural setting of Ayodhya, he wrote: 'The country yielded good crops, was luxuriant in fruit and flower, and had a genial climate. The people had agreeable ways, were fond of good works, and devoted to practical learning. There were above 100 Buddhist monasteries, and more than 3,000 Brethren who were students of both the "Vehicles"'.[17] Hiuen Tsang who visited Ayodhya during the seventh century CE, found 1,000 monasteries and 3,000 monks studying books of both the 'Great' (Mahayana) and the 'Little' (Hinayana) Vehicles of Buddhism.[18]

Saketa is mentioned in Jain literature as well. The Adipurana and Vividha Tirthakalpa, texts of the early medieval period, describe it as one of the greatest centres of Jain religion. It is also stated that the fourth Jain Tirthankara had received his first alms at Saketa. The place was also visited by Vardhamana Mahavira, the twenty-fourth Tirthankara who was a contemporary of Lord Buddha and the founder of Jainism.[19] Ayodhya holds significance in Jainism as the birthplace of Tirthankaras like Rishabhdev, Shri Ajitnath, Shri Abhinandannath, Shri Sumatinath and Shri Anantnath. Jain literature refers to Ayodhya by various names such as Vinita, Saket, Koshla, Ixvakubhumi, Rampuri and Vishakha in different contexts. In the Aadi Purana, Digambar mok Jinasena notes, 'Aribhih yoddhumna shakya-Ayodhya' signifying that the city was 'invincibile, hence Ayodhya'. Described as a city with splendid houses adorned with flying banderols on their rooftops, it is referred to as Saket because of this feature. The name Vinita is derived from the humility of the 'Ayodhyavasi' or residents. Vimalsuri in Paumchariu attributes the founding of Ayodhya to Kuber after the destruction of Kalpvrix. The inhabitants' staple food being sugarcane (Iakh or Ixu) led to the clan being named Ixvaku, and the place became Ixubhum.[20]

The Gupta period from the late third century CE was a golden age for Ayodhya. The Gupta age is characterized by the revival of Hinduism.[21] In the fifth century CE, under the Gupta rule, Saketa underwent a transformation, becoming known as Ayodhya and gaining recognition as the precise location of the capital of the Iskhavaku kings during the Treta Yuga. Prabhavatigupta, the half-sister of Kumaragupta I was one of the earliest devotees of Ram, the avatar of Vishnu. It is also believed that Gupta king Skandagupta (455–467 CE) shifted his capital from Pataliputra to Ayodhya, as the former was ravaged by flood.[22] The Gupta rulers also encouraged the identification of Saketa as Lord Ram's Ayodhya.

Ayodhya declined as a political and economic power centre in the sixth century CE after the fall of the Gupta empire and the invasion of the Huns. However, by this time, Ayodhya had become a major pilgrimage centre due to its association with Lord Ram and the Ramayana. From the fifth to the eleventh century CE, Ayodhya was one of the principal religious Vaishnavite centres. In this period, many temples were built that were dedicated to Lord Vishnu; these also had statues of Lord Ram. During the reign of Harshavardhana (636–640 CE), Chinese explorer Hiuen Tsang visited India and gave a description of Ayodhya which comprised of many Buddhist monasteries and ten 'deva' temples. The very fact that Hiuen Tsang noticed the existence of what he called deva temples shows how prominent these temples were—that they were noticed by an individual of another faith. Although Hiuen Tsang did not specifically mention about the particular existence of a Ram temple at Ayodhya, it was he who spread the Ramayana from India to China.[23] Another mention of Ayodhya is found when King Yashovarman ascended the throne of Kannauj—which was another important kingdom of the Gangetic plains—in eighth century CE. He visited Ayodhya and built a temple there. In ninth century CE, Kannauj came under the rule of Pratiharas. Coins discovered from Hatia near Ayodhya suggest that Pratihara kings ruled over Ayodhya and that it was a flourishing city.[24]

CHRONICLES OF THE MEDIEVAL RAJ

During the reign of the Gahadavala dynasty in the eleventh and twelfth century in Kannauj, Ayodhya rose to become one of the most prominent pilgrimage centres. Gahadavala king Chandradeva (1072–1096 CE) was the most important ruler of this dynasty. A copper plate inscription suggests that Chandradeva visited Ayodhya (also known as Uttara Kosal) in 1093 on the occasion of a solar eclipse and took a holy bath on the confluence of Sarayu and Ghaghra rivers. He then worshipped various deities such as Surya and Siva. He probably built a Vaishnava temple at Ayodhya and installed an image of Vishnu in it calling it Chandrahari, named after himself.[25] He is also said to have protected the sacred cities of Ayodhya and Kashi.[26]

An inscription of King Govindachandra, the grandson of Chandradeva, shows that Ayodhya was a prominent pilgrimage site, along with Kashi. Govindachandra's subordinate Samanta Ananyachandra built a magnificent temple dedicated to Lord Vishnu at Ayodhya.[27] Govindacharya also dedicated an image of Vishnu called Vishnu Hari at Ayodhya after his own name.[28]

Jayachandra, the last Gahadavala emperor of Kannauj, also built a temple dedicated to Lord Vishnu at Ayodhya. The temple became known as Treta Ke Thakur indicating that the temple was dedicated to Lord Ram, son of Dashrath. Lord Ram was already regarded as an incarnation of Lord Vishnu. It is suggested that the same temple became known as Ram Janmasthan temple. The temple became a significant Vaishnavite shrine attracting pilgrims from all over and continued to be a great pilgrimage for Hindus and others alike.[29]

ISLAM INVADES THE SHORES OF SARAYU

After the defeat of Jayachandra of Kannauj in 1193 CE, Ayodhya came under the Delhi Sultanate. In 1198, Muhammad Ghori accompanied by Makhdum Shah Juran Ghori attacked Ayodhya and occupied it. It is believed that Makhdum Shah destroyed many places of worship in the city.

From the thirteenth century onwards, Ayodhya remained an important place under the Delhi Sultanate, and later became the provincial capital of Awadh. Under the Delhi Sultanate, it remained a major administrative and military station from where troops could be sent to Bengal in the east. Ayodhya was of strategic geographical importance to the rulers, given its proximity to the eastern part of the country. For instance, the second ruler of the Delhi Sultanate, Iltutmish, appointed his eldest son, Nasiruddin Mahmud, as the governor of Awadh in 1226. Ayodhya continued to remain a city of significance during Balban's reign, and it continued to occupy an important position during the Khalji and the Tughlaq dynasties as well. Towards the end of the Tughlaq

Dynasty, the control of Delhi over Ayodhya became lax. After Taimur's invasion in 1398, the Delhi Sultanate broke into several parts, and Awadh came under the rulers of Sharqi dynasty which ruled from 1394–1478 CE. During the reign of Sharqi dynasty, Awadh no longer remained a major centre of political power in the region; that position was now accorded to Jaunpur. It was during the Lodhi dynasty that Awadh was reinstated as an important political and military station.[30]

According to several political and religious sources, Ayodhya during the Sultanate period remained not only a growing centre of political and commercial activity but also of religious significance. The period of the rise of Delhi Sultanate coincided with the emergence of the Bhakti movement. It is believed that three temples devoted to Lord Ram were built in Ayodhya during the twelfth century, but, unfortunately, there are no traces of them that can be seen in the present times.[31] By the fourteenth century, periodical fairs were organized in Ayodhya that served both commercial and religious ends. The most important festival was undoubtedly the birth anniversary of Ram, which attracted a large crowd at the Ram *janmasthan* (birthplace of Ram).[32]

During the Mughal era, a large number of Hindu temples were destroyed. This finds mention in several texts. In 1528–29, Mir Baqi Mir, a general of the first Mughal emperor Babur destroyed the temple at the Ram Janmasthan in Ayodhya and in its place built the Babri Masjid. Tulsidas, who wrote the Ramcharitamanas was a contemporary of Babur. In his Tulsidasa Dohashataka, he bemoaned the destruction of the Ram temple and wrote: 'The Yavanas (foreigners) filled with anger ridiculed the mantras, Upanishads, Brahmanas and Puranas; after cutting the tuft of hair and yagopavit (sacred thread of Brahmins).' This is followed by a verse that, in original, goes: '*Bhad hari bhagaye desh se, Tulsi kathin kujog.*' It means, 'They expelled the followers of Hari from their homes. Tulsi says this is a bad time.' The verses go on to say that 'Babur came with a sword in hand in the summer months of Vikram Samvat 1585 (1528 AD) and created havoc (*anarth*). The beautiful Ram Janmasthan temple was ruined and a mosque built; Tulsi felt aggrieved.' Tulsidas further says, 'Where there was a temple on Ram's birthplace, in the middle of Awadh, Mir Baqi built a mosque.'[33]

The later descendants of the Mughals also destroyed temples in Ayodhya. However, despite this destruction, Ayodhya continued to remain an important pilgrimage site for Hindus; this was also recognized in major Persian texts of the period. Abul Fazl in *Ain-i-Akbari* wrote that the town of Awadh was one of the most holy places in ancient India, being the capital seat of Lord Ram, who combined spiritual sovereignty with earthly kingship.[34]

After the destruction of the Ram Janmasthan Temple by Babur, the Hindus did not cease to relinquish their claim on Ram Janmabhoomi. Mughal emperor Akbar recognized such claims and allowed the construction of a *chabutara* (platform) or a raised platform in the courtyard of the mosque, allowing Hindus to worship there.[35]

The pace of the destruction of temples picked up during the reign of Aurangzeb; this has been mentioned in many accounts of that period. *Maasir-i-Alamgiri* by Saqi Musta'd Khan states: 'Large number of the places of worship of the infidels and great temples of these wicked people have been thrown down and desolated. Men who can see only the outside of things are filled with wonder at the successful accomplishment of such a seemingly difficult task. And on the sites of the temples, lofty mosques have been built.'[36]

After the death of Aurangzeb, many provincial heads proclaimed semi-independence. One such example was that of the Nawabs of Awadh who were comparatively tolerant; Nawab Saadat Khan Burhan Ul Mulk founded the independent Awadh kingdom in 1724 CE after breaking away from the Mughal Empire. Under Shuja-ud-Daula (1754–1775), Awadh evolved into a stable political and economic unit. Nawabs of Awadh initially settled in Faizabad, which was situated around 10 km from Ayodhya, and made it their capital. Due to the religious tolerance of the Nawabs, many temples, shrines and living establishments were either re-established, replaced or new ones were founded.

Rulers from other regions, such as Ahilyabai Holkar of Indore, the Rajas of Jaipur, the Bhosle of Nagpur and many others, too built temples here Hanumangarhi, built in 1774 CE was constructed on 20 acres of land given by Nawab Shuja-ud-Daulah.[37] A decree bearing the personal signature of Nawab Shuja-ud-Daula, granting a piece of land in Ayodhya to a Hindu hermit named Abhai Ram Bairagi for the establishment of a garden and the construction of a *dharmashala* (religious shelter) for the benefit of Hindu pilgrims, has been safeguarded.[38]

ANNEXATION OF AYODHYA BY BRITISHERS

Under the Nawabs, Awadh flourished into a wealthy kingdom. Hence, from the eighteenth century, it aroused the interests of the Britishers in India. Nawab Shuja-ud-Daula had entered into treaties with the British East India company regarding the number of armed personnel. It was during the tenure of Nawab Asaf-ud-Daula that Britishers emerged as dominant political players in the affairs of Oudh and signed a more exploitative treaty with the Nawab. This led to a diplomatic and political isolation of the region. A permanent resident of the Company was also stationed at Awadh. Later, Nawabs, such as Saadat Ali Khan, became puppets in the hands of the British and, through a treaty in 1801, large territories were ceded to them. High revenues were also extracted from Awadh.[39]

In 1856, the region was annexed into the territories of the British East India Company by the orders of Governor General Lord Dalhousie under the terms of the Doctrine of Lapse on the grounds of alleged internal misrule. Thus, the region came to fall directly under British rule.

Even during the British rule, Ayodhya continued to find its significance in Hinduism. There were times in history when its political significance was on the rise, as well as on the wane. But its spiritual significance has been constant. Ayodhya continued to be religiously, spiritually and culturally significant for the people even when the Ram Janmasthan Temple was destroyed by Muslim invaders almost 500 years ago and a disputed mosque was built on its ruins. Since then, the Hindus had been striving to reclaim their sacred space. This process gained momentum in the nineteenth century, continued through the next century and acquired the form of a movement that was to be a defining moment in the annals of modern Indian history.

2

THE LONG HAUL

The rulers in Indian history who came to reign over Ayodhya never might have imagined the repercussions of their actions. One can wonder if they ever knew that their stance to resolve a mere land dispute would have manifold effects, that it would change the course of history and the idea of secularism in India, and the roller-coaster ride that would become of Hindu–Muslim relations in the country. The quest for Hindu rights over Ram Janmabhoomi consumed centuries worth of legal drama, social upheaval and, at graver times, religious animosity.

AYODHYA CONFLICT: THE BEGINNINGS

The formal documentation of Ayodhya Ram Janmabhoomi conflict only began from nineteenth century onwards. However, scattered records claim that there had been around 64 conflicts between Hindus and Muslims over the disputed site since the temple was razed. In 1822, Hafizullah,

a superintendent of Faizabad law court submitted a document
which claimed that the mosque constructed by Babur was
situated at the birthplace of Ram, son of Raja Dashrath, and
was adjacent to the site of Sita Ki Rasoi.[1]

Subsequently, around three decades later in 1852, the
Nirmohis, a Hindu sect based at Ram Ghat and Guptar Ghat,
asserted ownership of the Babri Masjid. They argued that
the mosque occupied the site where the Ram Janmasthan
temple had been demolished by Babur. These claims led to
the violent conflict of 1853–55 when Maulvi Ghulam Hussein
with around 400–500 followers, charged on the 70-ft-high
Hanumangarhi from the Babri Masjid located less than a
kilometre away. They were pushed back by Bairagi sadhus
who chased them back up to the Babri Masjid where, in the
bloodshed, 75 Muslims and 11 Hindus were killed.[2] After few
months, a group of fundamentalists led by Maulvi Amir Ali,
a pirzada of Amethi, attacked Hanumangarhi. He made an
attempt to take over the temples at Ayodhya. The last Nawab
of Awadh, Wajid Ali Shah, sent his army to suppress the
attack, where Amir Ali's supporters were killed in a direct
fight in the Barabanki district.[3]

The Hindus continued to lay claim to the site claiming it
to be the birthplace or janmasthan of Lord Ram. In November
1858, a Nihang Sikh Fakir Khalsa from Punjab along with
25 fellow Sikhs captured the mosque at Ayodhya, placed
an idol in its central part near the pulpit and established a
nishan (flag) outside the mosque. He performed puja inside
the shrine and wrote 'Ram Ram' with coal in all parts of
the mosque.[4] *Thanedar* (police officer) of Awadh, Sheetal
Dubey, in his report dated 28 November 1858 provides the
first available record on contestation taking place between

Hindus and Muslims at the site.[5]

On 30 November 1858, the *mutawalli* (manager or custodian) of Babri Masjid, Muhammad Afzal, petitioned to the British government to oust the Sikh from the mosque. It is significant that, in the first petition, the disputed structure was referred to as Masjid Janmasthan (Birthplace Mosque). The English translation of the first appeal said: 'In a recent incident one Nihang Sikh, resident of Punjab Sikkhan, a government employee, is creating riot of Janmasthan Masjid situated in Oudh'.[6] The application also said that a chabutara was constructed inside the Babri Masjid. The Nihang Sikh was ousted from the mosque in December 1858. After a series of conflicts, in 1859, the colonial British administration put a fence around the site, denominating separate areas of worship for Hindus and Muslims.

In 1860, Mir Rajib Ali, *khatib* (preacher) of Babri Masjid filed an application in the court of the deputy commissioner of Faizabad asking for the chabutara that had been constructed inside the Babri Masjid to be demolished. This complaint was reiterated in 1861 where the complainant stated that the chabutara built near Babri Masjid at the Janmasthan had not been removed. In 1866, Muhammad Afzal, the mutawalli, filed another complaint saying that the Bairagis had constructed a *kothri* (cell) 'in an illegal manner within a few hours inside the compound of the mosque'. Afzal wanted the kothri to be dismantled and the Masjid 'protected from the fury of the Bairagis'.[7]

In 1873, an order was passed for the removal of an idol (Charan Paduka) that was said to have been created in the disputed building. Four years later, in 1877, Muhammad Ashgar requested the implementation of this order stating that the Charan Paduka had not been removed and also that Mahant Baldeo Das had made a *chulha* (earthern stove) within the compound of the disputed structure. In 1882, Muhammad Ashgar filed a complaint against Raghubar Das, *mahant* (priest) of the Janmasthan, claiming rent for the use of the chabutara near the gate of the Masjid. The complaint said that, during Mela Kartiki and Ram Navami, as well as on other days, shops of flowers were put up on the chabutara and in the courtyard on rent. The suit of Muhammad Ashgar was dismissed by a trial court. Hari Kishan, sub judge of Faizabad, stated that Ashgar, while claiming the rent for the use of the chabutara and the *takht* (bed), had admitted that these were in possession of Raghubar Das.[8]

In 1883, Muhammad Ashgar filed another application as the mutawalli and Khatib of Babri Masjid, claiming that he was entitled to get the wall of the mosque white-washed but was being obstructed from doing so by Mahant Raghubar Das, who he claimed had the right only to the chabutara and Sita Ki Rasoi. Faizabad assistant commissioner's order passed in January 1884 restrained Raghubar Das from carrying out repairs in the inner and outer parts of the compound. The order also advised Muhammad Ashgar not to lock the outer door of the mosque and leave it open. Sometimes thereafter, Raghubar Das filed a suit seeking permission to construct the Ram temple over the chabutara at the Janmasthan, measuring 21 ft by 17 ft. He also attached a map with the complaint. In response to the suit, Muhammad Ashgar filed a written statement on 22 December 1885, stating that Babur had constructed the mosque. The statement said that no one else could claim the right of construction there. Until the king or any of his successors had given permission to give away any part of the land, Mahant Raghubar Das could not become the owner of the land.[9]

The Gopal Sahai Amin Commission was appointed by the Court of Faizabad to prepare a map of the site after conducting a spot inspection. A report was submitted on 6 December 1885 which later came to be of great significance. It showed that Sita Ki Rasoi, the chabutara, the Janmasthan and the enclosure of the disciple of the mahant were all situated within the boundary wall of the site where the Masjid stood. Beyond the boundary wall, just adjacent to it was a deep depression pathway on all the four sides (*parikrama*) of the pilgrims. In this way, the entire area enclosed by the parikrama, as per the report, was the sacred Janmasthan.[10]

The case was heard by Sub Judge, Faizabad, Pandit Hari Kishan. On 24 December 1885, Pandit Kishan made a spot inquiry of the mosque and observed that, in 1855, after the fight between Hindus and Muslims that ensued from the attack led by Maulvi Amir Ali, a boundary wall was constructed to avoid future disputes, so that Muslims could worship inside the wall and Hindus outside the wall. He observed that the chabutara and the land which was situated outside the boundary wall belonged to Hindus. However, the sub judge denied permission to Raghubar Das to construct a temple and noted:

> If a temple is constructed on the chabutara on such a place, then there will be the sound bells of the temple and the *shankh* (conch shells) when both Hindus and Muslims pass from the same way, and if permission is given to Hindus for constructing temple, then one day or the other, a criminal case will be started and thousands of people will be killed.[11]

The case of Raghubar Das was also heard by District Judge,
Faizabad, Col F.E.A. Chamier. He also visited the site and,
in his judgment of March 1886, stated that it was 'most
unfortunate that a masjid should have been built on land
specially held sacred by the Hindus'. However, the judgment
stated that as that event occurred 356 years ago, it was too
late to remedy the grievance and 'all that can be done is to
maintain the parties in status quo'.[12]

On 1 November 1886, the officiating judicial
commissioner, W. Young, delivered his judgment noting that
the Hindus of Ayodhya wanted to create a new temple over
the chabutara and that this spot was situated on the precinct
of the grounds surrounding a mosque erected some 350 years
ago 'owing to the bigotry and tyranny of Emperor Babur, who
purposely chose this holy spot, according to Hindu legend,
as the site of his mosque'.[13] Young also observed that Hindus
had very limited rights of access to certain spots within the
precincts adjoining the mosque. Young, too, was against any
change in the status quo.

In 1902, the district administration placed markers for
all important places of Ayodhya. The first stone marker was
fixed in front of the eastern entrance of the disputed mosque
as 'No. 1 Ramajanmabhoomi'.[14]

On 20 and 21 November 1912, the first riots were
recorded in Ayodhya and Faizabad on the issue of cow
slaughter on the occasion of Bakr-id. A letter from R. Burn,
chief secretary, government of the United Province, to the
secretary to the government of India, home department,
dated 25 January 1913, stated that one perpetual cause of
friction was the existence of a mosque on the traditional site
of Ram's birthplace.[15]

On 18 July 1915, the lieutenant governor of United Province visited Faizabad to find a solution acceptable to the Hindus and the Muslims on the issue of cow slaughter in Ayodhya and observed that it was very difficult for anyone who was not a Hindu to appreciate the reverence which the Hindus felt for the holy ground of Ayodhya.[16]

In March 1934, riots again broke out in Ayodhya at the time of Bakr-id. According to the details of the incident provided by the commissioner of Faizabad to the chief secretary of the United Provinces, the immediate provocation was the performance of cow sacrifice in nearby Shahjahanpur. Meanwhile, in Ayodhya, a large crowd of Bairagis attacked the Babri Masjid. Upon hearing this news, the deputy collector reached the scene with five policemen and reported that the Bairagis had done considerable damage to the Masjid. In April 1934, chief secretary to the government of the United Provinces, H. Bomford, informed secretary to the home department, M.G. Hallett, that orders were issued for the imposition of a punitive police force at the expense of the Hindu inhabitants of Ayodhya. A fine of ₹85,000 was imposed on the Hindus to be given as compensation to the Muslims. This eventually aroused considerable resentment amongst the Hindus.[17]

In 1948, Muhammad Ibrahim, inspector of waqf, filed a report in regard to the Babri Masjid confirming that tensions continued to persist at the site. In the same year, Muhammad Ibrahim presented another report wherein he described his visit to Ayodhya. He mentioned that a Hindu saint Baba Sukhdas had visited Ayodhya a few months earlier and, while addressing the Bairagi sadhus and the Hindu priests, said that Ramayana *paath* (recital) should be done at the birthplace of

Lord Ram. After this, hundreds of Hindu saints assembled at the Janmasthan and the recitation of Ramayana paath went on for weeks.[18]

Thus, we see that Hindus had started to reclaim the site of Ram Janmasthan, which has been documented in many official documents from the period of the British rule. After India achieved independence, this Hindu struggle for claiming the sacred land of the birthplace of Ram at Ayodhya not only continued, it picked up pace during the decade of the 1980s. The main events of the Ayodhya dispute post-Independence and the related struggle of the Hindus to reclaim their sacred spot has been discussed in detail in a subsequent section. Before that, however, it is imperative to mention the multiple sources that shed light on the fact that Babri Masjid was indeed built on the remains of a demolished temple in Ayodhya.

SOURCES OF A DEMOLISHED TEMPLE IN AYODHYA

The Hindu claims over the disputed land find support in an array of literary sources, originating from Hindu, Persian, Urdu and foreign accounts. These early sources talk of the existence of a Ram temple at the site where the Babri Masjid was built after the temple's demolition. Most of these sources were written during the times of the Nawabs of Awadh. Apart from these sources, we also come across the accounts of the foreign travellers and the British administrators that mention the Babri Masjid being built at the site of the Ram Janmasthan temple.

PERSIAN AND URDU SOURCES

The *Jannah al-Mashriq wa Matla 'an Nur al-Mashriq*, retitled *Al-Hind-u fi al-'Ahd al-Islami* is an Arabic source which was translated into Urdu under the title *Hindustan Islami Ahd Mein*. The introduction of the book makes a reference to the destruction of a temple and the construction of a mosque at Ayodhya thus:

> And among them is the great mosque that was built by the Timurid King Babur in the sacred city of Ayodhya. It is believed that Rama Chandra considered to be the manifestation of God was born here. There is a long story about his wife Sita. There was a big temple for them in this city. At a certain place, Sita used to sit and cook food for her consort. Well, the said king Babur demolished it and built a mosque at that very place with chiselled stone.[19]

The *Tarikh-i-Awadh* written by Muhammad Najmul Ghani Khan Rampuri in 1919 stated that:

> At Ayodhya, where there stood the temple of Ramchandra Ji's Janmasthan, there is Sita ji ki Rasoi adjacent to it. King Babur got a magnificent mosque built there... Till date the mosque is called Masjid-i-Sita Ki Rasoi. And that temple is extant by the side. Babur built the temple by demolishing the Janmasthan and used it in his mosque the stone of same Janmasthan.[20]

The *Diya-i-Akhtar* by Haji Muhammad Hasan written in 1878 stated, 'Sayyid Musa Ashiqan built a mosque after levelling down Raja Ramachandra's palace and Sita's kitchen by the order of Zahir ud din Babur, king of Delhi.' This source also mentions that Aurangzeb built another mosque at the same place.[21]

Afzal-ut-Tawarikh, the second volume of *Ahsan-ul-Tawarikh* written by Munshi Ram Sahae Tamanna in 1879 describes the mosque built by Babur at Ayodhya as '*masjid-i-Janmasthan*' (literally meaning 'mosque of the birthplace').[22]

Tawarikh-i-Awadh is a work by Shaykh Azamat Ali Kakorawi which was completed in 1869 but came to light around 1986. One of its sections was published in 1987, and its opening paragraph reads:

> According to old records, it has been a religious rule with Muslim rulers, after the triumph of Sayyid Salar Masud Ghazi, to build mosques, monasteries and inns, spread Islam and put a stop to the blasphemous practice wherever they found manifestations. Accordingly, even as they cleared up Mathura, Brindavan etc. from non-Islamic practices, the magnificent Babari mosque (masjid-i-sarbaland-i-babari) came up in 923 AH under the patronage of Sayyid Musa Ashiqan in the Janmasthan temple in Faizabad–Awadh which was a great place of idol worship and the capital of Rama's father... Among the Hindus it was known as Sita Ki Rasoi.[23]

A Persian work of the early nineteenth century attributed to a Muslim saint Mawlawiyah 'Abdu'l Karim who belonged to the line of Sayyid Mir Musa Ashiqan at whose insistence Babur is said to have ordered replacing the temple in Ayodhya by a mosque, carries an account of how Babur decided and proceeded to demolish the Ram temple and built the mosque on its site under the influence of Sayyid Musa Ashiqan.[24]

A statement by Nizamu'd-Dawlah, the Kashmir ambassador to the court of Awadh in a statement in *Awadh Akhbar* in 1876 wrote that that there was indeed a temple at the birthplace of Maharaja Ramachandra (referring to King Ram or Lord Ram), and this was confirmed by the construction of a mosque on the same site by Babur Shah.[25]

The *Gumghasta Halat-i-Ajodhya Awadh*, where the title literally refers to the 'forgotten events of Ajodhya Awadh' by Maulvi Abdul Karim, imam of Babri Masjid cited several contemporary sources. This work was translated by his grandson in 1979. The translated work retained the section pertaining to the destruction of the temple at Janmasthan and the construction of a mosque in its place. However, when the second revised Urdu edition was published in 1981, this section was strangely omitted.[26]

Accounts of Foreign Travellers and British Administrators

Between 1608 and 1611 CE, William Finch visited India and, during his time in Ayodhya, he noted the deep reverence of Hindus for the city believed to be the birthplace of Ram. Arriving nearly 80 years after Babur, Finch attested to the continued active Hindu presence at the site. Notably, in his observations, Finch made no reference to Muslims engaging in *namaz*, prompting speculations about the possibility that the mosque may have been abandoned shortly after its construction was finished.

The account of Finch was also used by two travellers, Joannes de Laet and Thomas Herbert. Joannes de Laet was a Dutch geographer and director of Dutch West India Company. Describing the route from Agra to Jaunpur, he wrote:

From Cannove (Kannauj) to Lucanouw (Lucknow) is
30 cos. This is a great trading centre: thence to Oudee
(an ancient city, once the seat of Pathan Kings but now
almost deserted). Not far from this city may be seen
the ruins of the fort and palace of Ramchand, whom
the Indians regard as God... Pilgrims come to this place
from all parts of India and after worshipping the idol
take away with them some grains of charred rice as
proof of their visit.[27]

Joseph Tieffenthaler, an Austrian Jesuit, stayed in India
from 1743 till his death. He toured Awadh between 1766
and 1771. He is one of the foreign travellers who provide
a comprehensive account of Ayodhya. He was also the first
who refers to the destruction of a temple at Ram's birthplace
by a Mughal ruler. He mentioned about Hindus worshipping
a religious structure in the form of a *vedi* (cradle) in the
premises but did not write anything about Muslims offering
namaz in the mosque He also noted the large gathering of
Hindus on the auspicious occasion of Ram Navami (the day
when Ram was born). He wrote: 'Emperor Aurengzeb got
the fortress Ramcot demolished and got a Muslim temple,
with triple domes, constructed at same place. Others say
that it was constructed by "Babor".'[28]

In his *The East India Gazetteer* of 1828, Walter Hamilton
recorded the arrival of pilgrims who 'resort to this vicinity,
where the remains of the ancient city of Oude, and capital
of Great Rama are still to be seen'. He also mentioned
that religious mendicants 'walk around the temples and
idols, bathe in the holy ponds, and perform the customary
ceremonies'.[29]

Robert Montgomery, a British official, reported about the legend of King Vikramaditya who allegedly erected 360 temples at places sanctified by the deeds of Ram, Lakshman and Hanuman. Referring to the destruction of the temple by Babur or Aurangzeb, Montgomery wrote: 'The bigot, by whom the temples were destroyed, is said to have erected mosques on the situations of the most remarkable temples.'[30]

Patrick Carnegy, the first British commissioner and settlement officer of Faizabad wrote that at the time of the Muslim conquest, there were 'three important Hindu shrines...at Ayodhya. These were the Janmasthan, the Sargadwar Mandir and the Treta-ka-Thakur. On the first of these, Babur built the mosque which still bears his name... On the second, Aurangzeb did the same...on the third his predecessor built a mosque, according to the well-known Mahomedan principle of enforcing their religion on all whom they conquered.'[31]

The *Gazetteer of the Province of Oudh* prepared by W.C. Benett in 1878 noted that Ayodhya must have possessed a fine temple at Ram Janmasthan. This was so because many of the columns of the temple were still in existence and well preserved having been used by Muslims in the construction of the Babri Mosque.[32]

In his reports of 1862–63, British archaeologist Alexander Cunningham describes the ancient city of Ayodhya in great detail. He writes: 'Close by is the Lakshman Ghat, where his brother Lakshman bathed, and about one-quarter of a mile distant, in the very heart of the city, stands the Janam Asthan, or "Birth-place temple" of Ram.' Cunningham also wrote that there were several Brahmanical temples in Ayodhya but they were all of a modern date, saying, '...but there can be no doubt that most of them occupy the sites of more ancient temples that were destroyed by the Musalmans'.[33]

THE AYODHYA MOVEMENT POST INDIAN INDEPENDENCE

From the inception of India's independence, the reconstruction of temples have been intertwined with notions of national pride, symbolic cultural renewal and the preservation of heritage. The precedence was set by the initiatives taken by national leaders and the people to rebuild another sacred Hindu site which had suffered a similar fate—the Shri Somnath Jyotirlinga Temple in Gujarat, commonly referred to as the Somnath Temple. The genesis of this concept after Independence can be traced back to a pivotal moment on 12 November 1947 when Vallabhbhai Patel arrived in Junagadh. He witnessed the ruins of the Somnath Temple and subsequently set in motion the directive for its reconstruction. This act resonated with the collective aspiration of the people to restore the temple as a beacon of cultural continuity, embodying the nation's newfound independence and resurgent identity. Mahatma Gandhi bestowed his blessings upon this endeavour, concurrently suggesting that the construction funding should be sourced from public contributions, underscoring the principle that state funds should not be employed for the temple's restoration. Tragically, both Gandhi and Sardar Patel passed away, leaving the task of overseeing the temple's reconstruction to K.M. Munshi, who was the then minister for food and civil supplies. The process of revival was set in motion as the ruins were dismantled in October 1950.

The culmination of this endeavour occurred on 11 May 1951, when President Rajendra Prasad, despite Jawaharlal Nehru's expressed concerns, performed the deity installation or consecration ceremony for the temple. In his impactful speech, President Rajendra Prasad regarded Somnath as a symbol of ancient India's economic and spiritual prosperity, signifying the temple's reconstruction as a stride towards reclaiming India's past glory.[34]

Looking at it today, Sardar Patel's advocacy for the Somnath Temple's renovation stemmed from a complex interplay of motivations intertwined with India's struggle for independence and cultural preservation. Perceiving the temple as more than mere architecture, Patel saw it as a unifying emblem capable of weaving India's diverse cultural and religious fabric into a cohesive identity narrative. He called the reconstruction of the Somnath Temple a 'holy task' in which all should participate.[35]

The issue of Ram temple kept brewing in the background. However, the battle here was much fiercer and more complicated to be resolved in one blow. Within two years of India attaining independence, the battle for the construction of a Ram temple at the Ram Janmasthan in Ayodhya took an important turn. In 1949, devotees of Lord Ram submitted an application to the UP government seeking permission to construct a temple at the Ram Janmasthan. In a letter dated 20 July 1949, the then deputy secretary of the UP government sought the response of the Faizabad District Magistrate K.K.K. Nayar and the latter submitted his report on 10 October 1949. In the report, Nayar stated that the Hindu public had submitted the application to erect a big temple in place of a small one which existed at present. 'There is nothing in the way and permission can be given as Hindu population is very keen to have a nice temple at the place where Bhagwan Ramchandraji was born.'[36]

On 16 December 1949, Nayar in a letter to the home secretary in the UP government stated that a magnificent temple at the site was constructed by Vikramaditya. The temple was not only destroyed by Babur but the Babri Masjid was constructed on it and, in this process, the building material of the temple was used.[37] While correspondences were being exchanged between officials regarding the Ram temple and the Babri Masjid, a First Information Report (FIR) was filed by Senior Sub Inspector Ram Deo Dubey, in charge of the local police station in Ayodhya. The FIR mentioned that a group of 50–60 people had entered the Babri Masjid the previous night and placed an idol of Lord Ram in the mosque. It may be noted here that no Muslim came forward to lodge an FIR or any official complaint.[38]

Nayar wrote two letters dated 26 December and 27 December 1949, to Bhagwan Sahai, chief secretary in the UP government. In the letter dated 26 December, Nayar pointed to the 'immense public sympathy in support of the cause'. In the letter dated 27 December, Nayar said that the commissioner had given him and the superintendent of the police a scheme for removing the idol from the mosque. Nayar categorically stated that this idea of removing the idol was 'fraught with the gravest danger to public peace over the entire district and must lead to a conflagration of horror unprecedented in the annals of this controversy'. Nayar further stated in the letter that the Hindus, with no exception, were for keeping the idol in situ and were 'ready to die and kill for this cause'. He added: 'I shall also be unable to find in the district a Hindu, let alone a qualified priest, who will be prepared on any inducement to undertake the removal of the idol.'[39]

On 29 December 1949, Markanday Singh, the additional city magistrate of Faizabad-cum-Ayodhya ordered the attachment of the property under Section 145 Criminal Procedure Code and appointed Priya Dutt Rama, Chairman Municipal Board as receiver to take care of the property. Dutt took charge on 5 January 1950 and took steps to ensure that *bhog* (religious food offering) and puja continued at the site.[40]

On the developments happening in Ayodhya, Deputy Prime Minister (PM) Sardar Vallabhbhai Patel wrote a letter to the chief minister (CM) of UP dated 9 January 1950. Patel said that he realized there was a great deal of sentiment involved with the issue but 'such matters can only be resolved peacefully if we take the willing consent of the Muslim community peacefully with us'.[41]

On 16 January 1950, Gopal Singh Visharad filed a case with a civil judge in the district court of Faizabad, seeking permission to worship the deities installed at 'Asthan Janma Bhoomi'. An interim injunction restraining Muslims from removing the idols was granted. On 5 December 1950, Paramhans Ram Chandra Das filed a suit seeking permission for 'worship and darshan without any check, obstruction or interference'. On 1 February 1951, Faizabad civil judge consolidated the suits filed by Gopal Singh Visharad and Ram Chandra Das giving interim orders allowing devotees to worship keeping the inside area closed. On 3 March 1951, the High Court sealed the order announced by the civil judge.[42]

On 17 December 1959, on behalf of the Nirmohi Akhara, Mahant Raghunath filed a third suit with a civil judge in

the district court of Faizabad, seeking to remove Priya Dutt
Ram from the management of the 'temple' and take charge
himself. He had been appointed the custodian of the disputed
area in 1949.[43] On 16 December 1961, the UP Sunni Central
Waqf Board and others filed a suit against Visharad, seeking
'a decree for the delivery of possession of the mosque and
graveyard by removal of the idols and other articles'. On 6
April 1964, all the three case filed by Hindus along with the
one filed by the Waqf Board were consolidated as suit No.
12/1961. This suit became the main case in the dispute.[44]

ASI PROJECT ON 'ARCHAEOLOGY OF THE RAMAYANA SITES'

In 1975–76, a team of the ASI worked on a project titled
'Archaeology of the Ramayana Sites', which excavated five
Ramayana-related sites of Ayodhya, Bharadwaj Ashram,
Nandigram, Chitrakoot and Shringaverapura. At Ayodhya,
the ASI team found rows of pillar bases which must have
belonged to a building larger than Babri Masjid. However,
all technical facilities to the aforementioned ASI project
were withdrawn. The final report of the project was never
submitted and a preliminary report was published as late as
in 1989. In his book published in 2008, *Rama: His Historicity,
Mandir and Setu*, B.B. Lal wrote, 'Attached to the piers of
the Babri Masjid, there were twelve stone pillars, which
carried not only typical Hindu motifs and mouldings, but
also figures of Hindu deities'. The findings had revealed that
a large temple stood in alignment with the mosque since the
eleventh century CE.[45]

THE RAM TEMPLE MOVEMENT GAINS MOMENTUM

The movement for the construction of a Ram temple in Ayodhya was conceived in 1983 when the question of liberation of Ram Janmabhoomi was raised by Dau Dayal Khanna, a veteran Congress leader and a former UP minister in a Hindu *sammelan* (congress) in Muzzaffarnagar, UP. The meeting was also attended by Gulzarilal Nanda, who had served as the interim PM of India twice. Dau Dayal Khanna, who was the star speaker, spoke about building a Ram temple in Ayodhya in the presence of Nanda and Rashtriya Swayamsevak Sangh (RSS) people. He said that the temple should be built not only at Ayodhya but also at Mathura to mark Lord Krishna's birth and in Kashi for Lord Shiva. He emphasized that the temples should be rebuilt after demolishing the mosques.[46] Aged Congress leader Dau Dayal Khanna subsequently told Ashok Singhal—who later became the chief architect of the Ram Janmabhoomi Movement—that a Ram temple should be constructed in Ayodhya and for which a mass movement is needed. Khanna said to Singhal that he was now old and did not have the required organizational support and people with him, and asked him to start the movement since he had 'organizational support and thousands of activists'. Khanna also said, 'This movement will change the direction and nature of the cultural and political discourse of the country.'[47]

Ashok Singhal used to take advice from sadhus and saints and follow their guidance in his plan of actions. Singhal also made sure he kept sadhus at the front of the movement, while the implementation of their ideas was being taken care of by the Vishva Hindu Parishad (VHP) and RSS. One could say that the modus operandi of the movement was *'santon ka mantra aur VHP ka tantra* (ideas of saints and system of VHP)'.

On 7 and 8 April 1984, over 530 saints and sadhus took part in the First Dharm Sansad (religious congregation) in Delhi and unanimously resolved for the liberation of the birthplace of Lord Ram. Consequently, a meeting of the saints was held in Ayodhya on 18 June 1984 which declared Dau Dayal Khanna as the convenor of Ram Janmabhoomi Mukti Yajna Samiti (Ram Janmabhoomi Liberation Committee). At a meeting held again on 1 July 1984, Mahant Avaidyanath was declared as the president of the Committee.

On 25 September 1984, Shri Ram–Janaki Rath Yatra, a public procession, was started in Sitamarhi in Bihar to raise awareness among the people about the movement. On 7 October 1984, thousands of people assembled on the banks of Sarayu in Ayodhya and vowed for the liberation of the temple. They also demanded opening of the locks of the temple. On 14 October 1984, the Shri Ram–Janaki Rath Yatra received an unprecedented reception in Lucknow. The Rath Yatra programme was suspended in Ghaziabad on 31 October 1984, due to the assassination of the then Indian PM Indira Gandhi. Ashok Singhal at one place said during this yatra, 'Ram Temple was destroyed because Hindu society was divided and unorganized. We cannot guarantee that after the construction of the Ram Temple the temple would not be destroyed. The only guarantee could be an organized Hindu society.'[48] Another important leader Ramchandra Paramhans said, 'We have gained political freedom but culturally we are still not free. We will achieve cultural freedom when there would be a grand Ram temple in Ayodhya. This Ram temple movement would become a mass movement with the slogan of Jai Shri Ram, just as Vande Mataram was a famous slogan during the Indian freedom movement.'[49] Mahant Avaidyanath said, 'We have to establish a political power with Hindutva as its core ideology. We need political supremacy of the idea of Hindutva. We need to give up this idea of "*koi nrip hoi hume ka hani* (we don't care whosoever is the king)".'[50]

On 26 March 1985, Ram Janmabhoomi Mukti Yajna Samiti decided to enroll 50 lakh devotees of Lord Ram for liberating the Janmabhoomi. On 18 April 1985, Paramhans Ramchandradas declared that he would immolate himself if the locks were not opened.

The Shri Ram–Janaki Rath Yatra was restarted on 23 October 1985, on the occasion of Vijayadashami. On 31 October 1985, the Second Dharma Sansad was held in Udupi, Karnataka, which witnessed the participation of 851 saints. These saints planned for the upcoming challenges in the temple liberation struggle. On 19 January 1986, it was decided in a conference of saints held in Lucknow that the struggle for the liberation of the Ram temple would commence on the day of Shivaratri that year (8 March 1986). It was also decided that the locks would be broken if they were not opened by that time.[51]

On 1 February 1986, the district magistrate of then Faizabad (now Ayodhya) district ordered the opening the lock of the Ram Janmabhoomi on the plea filed by an advocate, Umeshchandra Pandey. After the opening of the locks, the Samiti started to plan the construction of a magnificent Ram temple there. Chandrakant Sompura from Karnavati (Ahmedabad) was selected as the architect for the proposed temple. A massive campaign was launched at the national level to lay the foundation stone of the temple. A small coupon with a picture of the proposed Ram temple on it was sold for ₹1.25 each to every individual who wanted to contribute in the construction of the Ram temple. This was accompanied by *shilapoojan* (worshipping of bricks) by groups of people collectively across the nation.[52]

Meanwhile, after the locks were opened, certain communal elements in Faizabad district started making attempts to organize Muslims against the construction of the temple. On 14 February 1986, a black day was observed by Muslims against the opening of the lock. Many temples in Kashmir were destroyed, and there was violence all around the country. On 15 February 1986, the Babri Masjid Action Committee (BMAC) was constituted. On 1 February 1989, over one lakh saints assembled on the occasion of Kumbha Mela and made a declaration that the foundation stone for the construction of the Ram temple would be laid on 10 November 1989. In this meeting, the replica of the Ram temple was showcased in the public for the first time.

In June 1989, a monumental decision was taken that would exercise a significant impact on India's political landscape. In a national executive meeting held in Palampur (Himachal Pradesh), the Bharatiya Janata Party (BJP) decided to support the Ayodhya movement. In this resolution, the BJP had stated that they would try to construct the proposed grand Shri Ram Temple at Ram Janmasthan in Ayodhya through mutual dialogue between the two communities or by enabling required legislation. 'The sentiment of the people must be respected and Ramjanmasthan handed over to the Hindus.'[53]

Richard H. Davis, in his 1997 book, *Lives of Indian*

Images, says the following to point to the fact that the BJP had borrowed the same strategy as that of K.M. Munshi in the case of the Somnath Temple. He writes, 'Like Munshi, they [BJP] claim that the restoration of a long-abandoned temple site is essential to the integrity of Hindu society, and have mobilised towards this end. Evoking Munshi's successful project, the BJP has portrayed its mobilisation to build a Ram temple atop the site of the Babri Masjid as a continuation of the "Spirit of Somanatha".'

On 10 November 1989, the foundation stone of the temple was laid by a Harijan, Kameshwar Chopal of Bihar. This was accompanied by the sound of conches and other musical instruments. Later, the *shilanyas* (laying the foundation stone) programme was carried out by saints and devotees by placing 200 bricks. At a meeting on the same day, the Margdarshak Mandal of the VHP decided that the natural culmination of the shilanyas programme was the construction of the temple. And for that purpose, saints would proceed for *kar seva* (religious voluntary labour) on 11 November 1989. On the said day, over 7,000 saints and devotees embarked from the banks of Sarayu to the temple site for kar seva, but they were stopped by the orders of the presiding district magistrate. That day, the saints decided to not resist.

In January 1990, it was decided in a conference of saints at Allahabad (now Prayagraj) to commence the work for the construction of a temple from 14 February 1990. Meanwhile, V.P. Singh, the new PM of India called the leaders of Ayodhya for talks in Delhi, asking for more time to discuss the matter with his colleagues. However, four months passed by, and no concrete steps were taken by V.P. Singh's government.

On 23 and 24 June 1990, the saints met at Haridwar and decided that kar seva for the construction of the temple would start from Devotthan Ekadasi as per the Hindu lunar calendar, which fell on 30 October that year. The BJP president, Lal Krishna Advani, openly committed his party's full support to VHP's decision to start the construction of the Ram temple. He warned that any attempt by the V.P. Singh government at the Centre to scuttle the planned construction of the temple would result in the 'greatest mass movement the country has ever witnessed'.[54] On 10 September 1990, Advani announced his plans for a 10,000-km rath yatra from Somnath to Ayodhya. On 25 September 1999, Advani's rath yatra began with massive support from followers, which was a clear indicator of the mood of the nation.

Meanwhile, Mulayam Singh Yadav, the then CM of UP declared that he would not let even a bird flutter over the proposed site of the kar seva (*'parinda bhi par nahi maar sakta'*).[55] Meanwhile, the rath yatra led by Lal Krishna Advani was stopped in its way as he was arrested in Samastipur, Bihar, on 23 October 1990. The arrest of Advani was condemned by common Hindus, resulting in bandhs all over the country in the next two days. The BJP also withdrew support to the Janata Dal government led by V.P. Singh.

There were tight security arrangements at Ayodhya, prohibiting the arrival of the kar sevaks. Despite this, thousands of kar sevaks reached Ayodhya and unfurled saffron flags at three domes of the disputed structure on 1 November 1990. On 2 November 1990, the government security personnel opened fire, killing several kar sevaks in the narrow lanes and bylanes of Ayodhya. Although the official death toll was stated at 18, it is believed that many more innocent and unarmed kar sevaks were killed in the firing by the security personnel. This incident was condemned nationwide, reflecting a feeling of anger against the action of the police. It would not be fallacious to call this killing of kar sevaks a massacre. This massacre also had a huge political fallout. The V.P. Singh government collapsed and Chandra Shekhar became the new Indian PM. In April 1991, Mulayam Singh Yadav also had to resign as the CM of UP. A Satyagraha was started in Ayodhya in December 1990 by the kar sevaks to register protest against the killings of their fellow kar sevaks and to demand justice for those who had sacrificed their lives.

The new Chandra Shekhar government made attempts to organize meetings between the VHP and the BMAC. As per the agenda of the meetings, Muslims would give up their claim to the site if it was proved that the disputed Babri structure was built after the demolition of the temple. Both the parties agreed to submit their respective evidence in writing to the minister of state for home affairs by 22 December 1990 and who would, in turn, exchange the same between the parties concerned by 25 December 1990. Both the parties would review these evidences and submit their comments back to the minister by 6 January 1991. Both the parties had to prepare their points of agreement and disagreement and send them to the parties concerned by 9 January 1991. They met again on 10 January 1991 in Gujarat Bhawan in New Delhi. In that meeting, it was decided that each side would nominate experts, after which they would meet on 24–25 January 1991 to assess the evidence. On 25 January 1991, experts from the Hindu side reached Gujarat Bhawan but none of the Muslim experts showed up. This sudden absence of the Muslim side led to a breakdown of negotiations.

The 1990s were a period of political instability at the Centre. In March 1991, the Chandra Shekhar government fell, and fresh elections to the Lok Sabha were announced. The election manifesto of the BJP made a commitment to building a Ram temple at the Ram Janmasthan in Ayodhya. After the general elections, the Congress Party formed a minority government at the Centre with P.V. Narasimha Rao as the PM.

In the UP legislative assembly elections, the BJP had captured power and Kalyan Singh became the CM of UP. In October 1991, the Kalyan Singh government decided to acquire 2.77 acres of land surrounding the disputed structure. However, this acquisition became a matter of judicial dispute and the Supreme Court of India ordered status quo on the acquired land.

In January 1992, leaders of the Ayodhya movement held two meetings with Kalyan Singh, the then UP CM, and in March 1992, the UP government handed over 48 acres of land to the Ram Janmabhoomi Nyas. Meanwhile S.B. Chavan, the then union home minister threatened to impose Article 356 or President's Rule in Uttar Pradesh.

In May 1992, the saints met at Ujjain, and it was decided that the kar seva would be resumed on 9 July 1992. On 9 May 1992, members of the Samiti met with P.V. Narasimha Rao regarding the construction of the temple and informed him of the kar seva. As planned, the kar seva started on the proposed date and rituals were performed in the premises of Ram Janmabhoomi. On 23 July 1992, Narasimha Rao called on the saints and asked for a time of four months; the kar seva was then suspended. Ashok Singhal, VHP general secretary, told the kar sevaks that the kar seva would resume in November 1992.

THE DEMOLITION OF THE DISPUTED STRUCTURE

The kar sevaks had started to reach Ayodhya in large numbers. By 3 December 1992, over 25,000 armed policemen were stationed in Ayodhya and over 12,500 kar sevaks were arrested. On 6 December 1992, in a sudden turn of events, the disputed Babri structure was razed to the ground by the kar sevaks. The entire structure made from mud and chalk was levelled by the crowd with axes, hammers and grappling hooks. Within the next five hours, the kar sevaks had demolished the disputed structure. An idol of Shri Ram Lalla was installed on a flat platform. The leaders made a desperate attempt to control the crowds. An announcement over the loudspeaker asked the kar sevaks to stop, to step back, but the orders and pleas had no effect.[56]

AFTERMATH OF THE DEMOLITION

At 5.00 p.m. on 6 December 1992, Kalyan Singh owned moral responsibility of the demolition and resigned as the CM of UP. A few hours later, the UP government was dismissed by the Centre and the state assembly was dissolved. Two FIRs were lodged at the Ram Janmabhoomi police station. The first was lodged against unknown kar sevaks. The second FIR named prominent names: Ashok Singhal, Giriraj Kishore, L.K. Advani, Murli Manohar Joshi, Vishnu Hari Dalmia, Vinay Katiyar, Uma Bharati and Sadhvi Ritambhara. On the basis of this FIR, L.K. Advani, Vishnu Hari Dalmia, Ashok Singhal, Murli Manohar Joshi, Uma Bharati and Vinay Katiyar were arrested on 8 December 1992 but were released on 10 January 1993 due to lack of evidence.[57] On 10 December 1992, five organizations—RSS, VHP, Bajrang Dal, Islamic Sevak Sangh and Jamait-e-Islami were banned under Unlawful Activities (Prevention) Act, 1967. The central government, in an arbitrary move, further dismissed the BJP governments in Himachal Pradesh, Rajasthan and Madhya Pradesh under Article 356 of the Constitution of India. However, in response to a petition seeking the right to perform puja at the contended site, the Allahabad High Court granted on 1 January 1993 the right to *darshan* (viewing) and to perform puja at the site.[58]

On 7 January 1993, the Narasimha Rao government issued an ordinance acquiring 67.7 acres of land (of the site and adjoining areas). Later, this was passed as a law—Acquisition of Certain Area at Ayodhya Act, 1993 to facilitate the acquisition of land by the central government. In 1994, the Supreme Court, by a majority of 3:2, upheld the constitutionality of the Acquisition of Certain Area at Ayodhya Act. The majority judgment by former Chief Justice of India J.S. Verma reasoned that every religious immovable property is liable to be acquired. The Supreme Court adjudged that offering namaz at a mosque was not integral to Islam unless that mosque had any particular significance in Islam.[59].

From 1993–2002, legal proceedings took place between various leaders associated with the Ram Janmabhoomi Movement. In February 2002, the VHP announced a new deadline of 15 March 2002 to start the construction of the Ram temple in Ayodhya. Kar sevaks gathered in large numbers.[60] The unfolding of the unfortunate and gory incident at Godhra in 2002 is known to everyone, where kar sevaks were burnt alive in the compartments of the Sabarmati Express train. The Godhra incident, as it came to be known, led to a feeling of angst amongst the Hindus of India. In a sense, the incident at Godhra also reignited the Hindu struggle for reclaiming their lost sacred site in Ayodhya.

This incident, at the start of the twenty-first century, once again led to the Ram Temple Movement gaining momentum. The frequency of the judicial proceedings were also about to increase. Subsequently, a few landmark judgments were pronounced that successfully bore to fruition the 500-year-old struggle for reclaiming the sacred Ram Janmabhoomi at Ayodhya. These historic judgments and how they exercised an impact on the Ram Janmabhoomi Movement is what constitutes the next chapter.

3

THE VERDICT

The Ayodhya dispute not only bore political implications but was also entangled in legal proceedings. The 'Acquisition of Certain Area at Ayodhya Act' has already been discussed in the previous chapter—how an Act was passed by the Centre for the acquisition of land in the disputed area in Ayodhya. Various writ petitions were filed, including the one by Ismail Farooqi in the Allahabad High Court, challenging various aspects of the Act. The Supreme Court, exercising its jurisdiction under Article 139A, transferred the writ petitions that were pending in the High Court.[1]

THE 2003 ASI REPORT

The Ayodhya title dispute case began in April 2002 led by the Lucknow bench of the Allahabad High Court. On 5 March 2003, the Lucknow bench comprising Justices Bhanwar Singh, S.R. Alam and Sudhir Narain directed the ASI to undertake excavation at the disputed site in Ayodhya to find out if a temple had existed at the site of the Babri Masjid.[2] The court said that the excavation should be carried within a month's time and the ASI report on the excavations should be submitted within a week of its completion. The Court directed ASI not to disturb the sanctum sanctorum where the statue of Ram Lalla was placed. 'The excavation should spare 10 sqm of the area (chabutra) where the statue of Ram Lalla is placed and where worshipping is carried out,' the order said.[3] The Court also asked the ASI to employ top experts for this work. It also asked Tojo India Vikas International (TIVI), a New Delhi-based Canadian company to assist the ASI. Tojo Vikas India (Pvt.) Ltd had earlier carried out a survey of the disputed area in Ayodhya with radar system and had submitted its report to the High Court.[4]

The ASI began its excavations on the orders of the High Court. On 12 March the ASI team convened with the parties involved in the Mandir–Masjid title dispute before the Allahabad High Court. They examined the area to be excavated, spanning approximately 5,000 sq. ft, ultimately reassuring all stakeholders of the genuine intentions of the ASI.[5] The ASI excavations at Ayodhya continued till 7 August 2003. In accordance with the direction of the High Court order, the ASI excavated 82 trenches to verify the findings of the radar survey conducted earlier.[6]

In August 2003, the 574-page ASI report consisting of written opinions, maps and drawings was opened before the Lucknow bench of the Allahabad High Court. The report said that there was archaeological evidence of a massive structure just below the disputed structure and evidence of continuity in structural activities from the tenth century onwards up to the construction of the disputed structure (Babri Masjid).

Among the excavation yields, it mentioned, were 'stones and decorated bricks, mutilated sculpture of a divine couple, carved architectural members including foliage patterns, *amalaka, kapotapali*, doorjamb with semi-circular shrine pilaster, broken octagonal shaft of black schist pillar, lotus motif, circular shrine having *pranjala* (watershute) in the north and 50 pillar bases in association with a huge structure.' The ASI report stated that archaeological evidence and other discoveries from the site were 'indicative of remains that are distinctive features found associated with the temples of north India'. Thus, the ASI report provided conclusive evidence of the fact that Babri Masjid was not built on virgin lands and was constructed after the demolition of a pre-existing temple on the same site.

JUDGMENT OF THE HIGH COURT

After seven years of initial proceedings, in 2010, the Allahabad High Court gave its verdict on the four petitions which had been clubbed together in this case. The three-judge bench comprising Justices S.U. Khan, Sudhir Agarwal and D.V. Sharma ruled in a majority judgment 2:1, that there be a three-way division of the disputed land—one-third for the Sunni Waqf Board, one-third for the Nirmohi Akhara and one-third to the party standing in for 'Ram Lalla' or the infant Lord Ram.

In an order that ran over 8,000 pages, the High Court said that the portion below the central dome, under which the idols of Lord Ram and other Gods were placed in a makeshift temple, belongs to Hindus. All three judges agreed with the same—that the portion under the central dome should be allotted to Hindus.

The Nirmohi Akhara, the judgment said, would get the Ram Chabutara and Sita Ki Rasoi. The court dismissed two major claims to the land—one filed in 1989 on behalf of Ram Lalla and the second by the Sunni Waqf Board filed in 1961.[7]

None of the three parties were satisfied by the judgment and appealed in the Supreme Court. Eleven other parties also filed special leave petitions before the Supreme Court challenging the 2010 Allahabad High Court verdict.[8]

However, the Supreme Court in May 2011 stayed the ruling of the High Court. A division bench of Aftam Alam and R.M. Lodha termed the High Court judgment as 'strange'. R.M. Lodha observed that 'a new dimension has been given by the High Court as the decree of partition was not sought by the parties. It was not prayed for by anyone. It has to be stayed. It's a strange order. How can a decree for partition be passed when none of the parties had prayed for it?'[9]

In 2017, Chief Justice of India J.S. Khehar suggested an out-of-court settlement among rival parties. A three-judge bench was constituted by the Supreme Court the same year to hear the civil pleas against the Allahabad High Court verdict. The hearings began the following year.[10]

THE 2019 SUPREME COURT AYODHYA VERDICT

In the wake of the historic Ayodhya title suit case judgment, the entire nation held its collective breath on the day prior to the judgment. So much so that every minute was being telecasted on television media, news websites and social media. People were glued to their TV sets and phones that provided hour-by-hour coverage of this landmark decision. The next day, the moment the Supreme Court ruled in favour

of Ram Lalla, the atmosphere in the country was electric
with anticipation.

Various security measures were put in place across the
country. In Delhi, barricades were put on roads leading to the
Supreme Court. Security outside the residences of Chief Justice
Ranjan Gogoi and Justices S.A. Bobde, D.Y. Chandrachud,
Ashok Bhushan and S. Abdul Nazeer, who were part of the
five-judge Constitution Bench and had to pronounce the
judgment on 9 November 2019, was also beefed up.[11]

In Ayodhya, security measures had been undertaken
from 8 November itself, a day before the judgment was to
be pronounced. Regular check posts were set up in the streets
and patrolling at roads was intensified, particularly during
night-time. As many as 45 CCTV cameras were installed
around important sites such as Hanumangarhi, Kanak
Bhawan, Dashrath Mahal and Ram Ki Paidi. The footage was
being fed into a centralized control room and monitored by
police officials. Section 144 was also imposed in Ayodhya to
be implemented until 28 December.[12]

The Supreme Court held the final and rather intensive
hearing spanning over 40 odd days (from 6 August 2019
to 16 October 2019). At 10.30 a.m. on the winter morning
of 9 November 2019, the judges announced a historic and
unanimous verdict clearing the way for the construction of
a Ram temple at the disputed site at Ayodhya and directed
the Centre to allot a 5-acre plot to the Sunni Waqf Board for
building a mosque. The main features of the Supreme Court
judgments were as follows:[13]

1. The Supreme Court ruled that the rightful possessor
    of the disputed 2.77-acre land was identified as Ram

Lalla Virajman, representing the infant Lord Ram and recognized as a juristic person. The directive mandated that the Centre must, within three months, devise a plan to establish a trust and transfer the land to this entity. '[It] shall make necessary provisions in regard to the functioning of the trust or body including...the construction of a temple and all necessary...matters,' the Supreme Court said in the order.

2. Both the Central and UP governments were directed to allocate 5 acres of land at an alternate site in Ayodhya for the Sunni Central Waqf Board to build a mosque. 'The land shall be allotted either by the Central government out of the land acquired under the Ayodhya Act 1993 or the state govt (UP) at a suitable prominent place in Ayodhya... The Sunni Central Waqf Board would be at liberty...to take all necessary steps for the construction of a mosque,' the Supreme Court said.

3. The Supreme Court said in its order that 'Hindu worship at Ramchabutra, Sita Rasoi and at other religious places...clearly indicated their open, exclusive and unimpeded possession of the outer courtyard.'

4. The court also said, 'Uttar Pradesh Sunni Central Waqf Board has failed to establish its case in Ayodhya dispute; Muslims have not adduced evidence they were in exclusive possession of the dispute site.'

5. The Court decreed that both the demolition of the Babri Masjid and the desecration of the Babri Masjid in 1949 were unlawful actions.

6. Overturning the 2010 Allahabad High Court decision

that divided the disputed site among the Sunni Waqf
Board, Ram Lalla Virajman, and Nirmohi Akhara,
the Supreme Court declared that the ruling 'defies
logic and is contrary to settled principles of law'. The
Supreme Court said that the 'three-way bifurcation
by the HC was legally unsustainable'. It said that 'the
high court was called upon to decide the question
of title, particularly in the suits... But the high court
adopted a path not open to it.'

7. The Court determined that the suit filed by Nirmohi
Akhara could not be sustained, as it lacked *shebait*
(manager of the temple) rights. Nevertheless, the
court decided that Nirmohi Akhara should be granted
suitable representation in the board of trustees.

8. The Court dismissed the Shia Waqf Board's petition
claiming that the disputed site belonged to them.

The Supreme Court also gave a message of unity and peace
to the nation in its judgment when it stated:

Above all, the law needs to be determined, interpreted
and applied in this case to ensure that India retains its
character as a home and refuge for many religions and
plural values. It is in the cacophony of its multi-lingual
and multi-cultural voices, based on a medley of regions
and religions, that the Indian citizen as a person and
India as a nation must realise the sense of peace within.
It is in seeking this ultimate balance for a just society
that we must apply justice, equity and good conscience.
It is in these situations, that courts are empowered to
ensure a just outcome by passing an order necessary to
ensure complete justice between the parties.[14]

RETURN FROM A CENTURIES-LONG VANVAAS

A five-century-old discord had been peacefully resolved, strengthening India's democracy. The Ayodhya Ram Janmabhoomi Temple verdict echoed like a clarion call across the pages of national and state newspapers, each headline encapsulating the essence of this historic moment. *The Times of India* succinctly declared, 'Ram Mandir Within Site', inspiring faith in the vision's realization. With a poetic touch, *Navbharat Times* echoed this sentiment with '*Mandir Wahi, Masjid Nayi* (Temple Stays, Mosque Replanned)', emphasizing the temple's rightful place in the hearts of millions. The *Hindustan Times* stated, 'Temple Set in Stone', capturing the immovable resolve of the decision. *The Indian Express* chose the words, 'Temple Gets Site, Mosque A Plot', reminding us of the pragmatic aspect of the verdict and the Sunni board's decision not to seek a review, thus ushering in a new era. *Dainik Bhaskar* proclaimed, '*Ram Lalla Hi Virajman* (Ram Lalla to be Seated)', highlighting the divine presence that now graced the site. *Dainik Jagran*, emphasizing the deity's significance, celebrated with a profound declaration, 'Shri Ram', accompanied by captivating illustrations of the deity and the temple. Gujarati newspaper *Divya Bhaskar*, exuberant and triumphant, chanted what means 'Victory to Ramchandra', acknowledging the end of a centuries-old dispute and a new beginning. These headlines, like verses in a song of unity, encapsulated the diverse emotions of a nation and its unwavering commitment to a brighter, harmonious future.

Hindu devotees rejoiced at the Supreme Court verdict. In Ayodhya, devotees went to temples and hailed *'Jai Shri Ram* (Hail Shri Ram)'. However, there was no celebratory frenzy, as political and religious leaders had asked the public to exercise restraint.[15] This was the case in almost every part of the country where the common Hindu devotee rejoiced but did not enter into a frenzied celebration. Peace was largely maintained throughout the length and breadth of the country. Many Muslim leaders urged the Muslim community to maintain peace and harmony. Maulana Mehboob Daryadi, general secretary of All India Ulema Council (AIUC) remarked: 'We are happy that the court hearing is finally over. We have been saying that we will accept whatever the verdict is. We accept the final order of the Supreme Court. We are also happy that the SC rejected the appeal of the Shia Waqf Board and Nirmohi Akhara. We accept that a five-acre land is given to the Sunni Central Waqf board to build the Masjid.' All India Muslim Personal Law Board (AIMPLB) member Maulana Sayyed Athar Ali said, 'We all should maintain law and order in the country and ensure that peace prevails. We all should accept the SC order.' Suhail Khandwani, managing trustee of the Mahim Dargah and trustee of Haji Ali Dargah said, 'It is a matter of pride that Indians have accepted the final order of the apex court. The SC has delivered a balanced verdict. This ruling is not in favour of any particular religion. The verdict has sent a message that India is above caste and creed.'[16]

In this post-verdict landscape, India discovered itself immersed in a fabric of narratives, echoing the diversity of its people and their opinions. Prime Minister Narendra Modi hailed the Ayodhya verdict, saying, 'The Honourable Supreme Court has given its verdict on the Ayodhya issue. This verdict shouldn't be seen as a win or loss for anybody. Be it Ram Bhakti or Rahim Bhakti, it is imperative that we strengthen

the spirit of Rashtra Bhakti. May peace and harmony prevail!'
Modi tweeted.[17] In the evening, Narendra Modi addressed
the nation and said that the Supreme Court heard everyone
with much patience and gave a unanimous verdict which has
shown its tremendous resolve. Additionally, he said:

> With today's verdict, the Honourable Supreme Court
> has given a message that even the toughest issues can be
> resolved within the framework of the Constitution and
> in spirit of the laws. We should learn from this verdict
> that even if there is some delay, we should remain
> patient. This is in everyone's interest. In every situation,
> our faith in India's constitution, India's judicial system
> must remain unwavering. This is very important.[18]

Prime Minister Modi noted that this decision has made it
incumbent upon all citizens to take their responsibility of
nation-building even more seriously. He laid emphasis on
the part that harmony, brotherhood, friendship, unity and
peace amongst the people is very important for the nation's
development. He then urged all citizens to work together to
achieve their goals and objectives.

L.K. Advani, a key architect of the Ram Janmabhoomi
Movement, wholeheartedly welcomed the historic Supreme
Court judgment on the Ayodhya issue, saying that he stood
vindicated and felt deeply blessed. 'I join all my countrymen
in wholeheartedly welcoming the historic judgment delivered
by the five-member Constitution Bench of the Supreme
Court today in the Ayodhya matter. I stand vindicated, and
feel deeply blessed, that the Supreme Court has given its
unanimous verdict paving the way for the construction of
a magnificent temple for Lord Ram at Ram Janmabhoomi

in Ayodhya,' he stated.[19] The VHP described the verdict as
a 'decisive step' towards the construction of a 'grand' Ram
temple and urged the central government to take speedy
steps on the directions issued by the Supreme Court. VHP
working president, Alok Kumar, said that the Supreme Court
order is a 'decisive step towards construction of grand Ram
temple in Ayodhya.' Mohan Bhagwat, the *sarsanghchalak*
(chief) of the RSS said that the RSS welcomed the verdict.
He also stated that the verdict should not be 'looked at as
a defeat or victory for anyone, rather something that would
strengthen the sense of unity in the country.'[20]

Apart from the BJP, many other political parties also
welcomed the verdict. The Congress Working Committee
passed a resolution accepting the Supreme Court verdict.
It also appealed to all parties and communities to abide by
secular values and the spirit of fraternity.

The decision on the proposed Ram temple's construction
was a momentous occasion that brought together people
from all walks of life, underlining the significance of unity
in diversity. It signified the triumph of dialogue, judicial
wisdom and collective determination, demonstrating India's
commitment to upholding its secular fabric while respecting
the cultural and religious sentiments of its citizens.

The positive narratives that emerged were multifaceted.
Many saw the judgment as a symbol of religious fulfilment,
bringing a sense of satisfaction among many Hindus and
fulfilling a long-held spiritual aspiration. It held historical
and cultural significance, signifying the restoration of
Hindu heritage and identity. At the same time, the verdict
became about something beyond a mere physical structure;
it symbolized the empowerment of a marginalized cultural

narrative and the healing of historical wounds.

On top of this, the judgment represented a significant legal victory, symbolizing national resolve and unity. It invoked a feeling of pride in the citizens owing to the nation's capacity to resolve complex historical and religious disputes. Discussions around the legal and constitutional aspects of the judgment highlighted the judiciary's role in interpreting intricate matters within the framework of the law.

The media played a pivotal role in shaping public perceptions, as their coverage and analysis steered the narrative around the verdict. Social media platforms became arenas for expressing opinions and sharing news, further amplifying the discourse.

Spiritual leaders too viewed the Supreme Court's judgment as a historic moment that brought joy and relief to people from both communities. Within hours of the judgment, they took to their social media accounts and addressed the public and media, sharing their views on the historic verdict. Spiritual leader Sri Sri Ravi Shankar, while addressing the media, said that the delivered judgment should be welcomed as a historic one, marking the conclusion of a long-standing struggle. He expressed his hope that the country would now move forward on the path of development.[21] Yoga guru Baba Ramdev had already emphasized earlier on Lord Ram's shared ancestry for both Hindus and Muslims, promoting unity and peace. He called for contributions from both communities to the temple's and mosque's construction. Baba Ramdev stressed the importance of upholding Lord Ram's values and avoiding actions that foster animosity.[22] Swami Avdheshanand Giri also took to Twitter (now X) with hashtag #acceptayodhyaverdict and expressed his admiration for the honourable Supreme

Court's decision by tweeting that restraint, peace, harmony, interfaith unity and reconciliation are the true essence of religion. He stated that Lord Ram personifies dharma, emphasizing the need for mutual love and unity among all.[23] In a recent interview, renowned spiritual guru Sadhguru Jaggi Vasudev also discussed the persistent landowning and title issues surrounding Lord Ram's legacy, even after thousands of years. He expressed the collective desire among Lord Ram's devotees to resolve these issues and commended the Supreme Court for its role in bringing closure to this matter. Sadhguru emphasized that while the land was mere 'real estate', the temple held a special place in the hearts of the devotees. He said that, for them, the land is sacred as it is recognized as Lord Ram's birthplace and that there had been no doubt about the presence of a temple at the birthplace.[24]

Analysing the verdict from an economic standpoint, the judgment was expected to boost tourism and revitalize the local economy of Ayodhya. This prospect was welcomed by those who saw it as an opportunity for prosperity, transcending religious affiliations.

On the political front, leaders from various parties and ideologies, including Amit Shah, Yogi Adityanath, Nitish Kumar, Akhilesh Yadav, Priyanka Gandhi, Randeep Surjewala and Nawab Malik, to name a few, urged the nation to accept the verdict. They emphasized the importance of communal harmony and the strengthening of democratic institutions. Former external affairs minister and senior Congress leader, Salman Khurshid, in an article, suggested that the judgment encouraged Muslims to embrace this as a moment of reconciliation rather than defeat, emphasizing the need for grace and unity. He also wrote that the court reinforced India's secular character, treating all citizens equally and suggested that the court judgment has nudged India to reconsider its approach to national life and move towards a common destiny after going through years of conflict.[25]

However, amidst these harmonious narratives, dissenting voices emerged. Inevitably, the Supreme Court decision also evoked memories of a similar historical debate surrounding the reconstruction of the Somnath Temple in Gujarat. Some believed that the verdict had the potential to rekindle historical animosities and communal tensions. Others argued that it diverted attention from pressing contemporary challenges, such as poverty, healthcare and education. However, the Ayodhya Ram Temple verdict, in fact, initiated conversations about closure and moving forward, signifying the nation's potential to heal and progress beyond this protracted dispute. The judgment aligned with the aspirations of many Indian Muslims, emphasizing social harmony and integration over religious concerns. The verdict aimed to shift the narrative away from identity politics and promote a more inclusive and forward-looking society.

In another corner of the media landscape, opinion pieces challenged the prevailing narrative of joy and triumph. Concerns were also raised about minority rights and the potential politicization of religious matters. Academician Pratap Bhanu Mehta, questioned the necessity and even the morality of constructing the temple.[26] He contemplated the futility of seeking justice through the lens of historical act of retaliation and revenge where no divinity could offer redemption.

In the judgment, the Supreme Court clearly pointed out that the Hindus had presented a stronger case, with the Waqf Board failing to establish exclusive possession of the disputed land. The court clarified that it did not rely on faith or majority–minority calculations but upheld the principle of equality before the law. The judgment rested on evidence of continuous worship, citing historical documents, travelogues and a report by the ASI that indicated the site's Hindu affiliation.

While a legally sound judgment provides the foundation for resolving disputes, the acceptance of such judgments by political leaders is crucial for ensuring closure and maintaining social harmony in a democracy. Syed Ghayorul Hasan Rizvi, chairman of the National Commission for Minorities pointed to this gap in acceptance long before the verdict. Speaking to *Rediff.com* in November 2018, he had said, 'The Muslim community is ready to give up the Babri mosque claim, but their leaders are not.'[27] To this constituency of hardline Muslim leaders, voluntary withdrawal from a claim of ownership over the disputed site risks being interpreted as the community giving into Hindu majoritarian hegemony. Glimpses of the same could be noted when, after the verdict, Journalist Rana Ayyub expressed uncertainty about whether to celebrate or mourn 'the silence' of Indian Muslim.[28] AIMIM (All India Majlis-e-Ittehadul Muslimeen) chief Asaduddin Owaisi expressed dissatisfaction with the Supreme Court's decision, rejecting the 5-acre land offer terming it as a 'charity' unacceptable to them (Muslims).[29] Sunni Waqf Board lawyer Zafaryab Jilani emphasized the mosque's invaluable nature as per the Sharia law and hinted at a potential review petition.[30]

Amidst these criticisms of the verdict, the majority of Muslims praised the Supreme Court's Ayodhya judgment for its amicable resolution and the avoidance of any violence.[31] Shia cleric Maulana Kalbe Jawad, too, humbly accepted the Supreme Court's verdict and encouraged putting the matter to rest. The decision, achieved through legal means, was seen as a balanced and peaceful solution that promoted harmony. Even before the judgment, Muslim leaders and intellectuals came together in a closed-door meeting organized by Navaid Hamid, president of the All India Muslim Majlis-e-Mushawarat, where they collectively emphasized the importance of respecting the Ayodhya verdict.[32] In a unanimous resolution, they pledged to uphold peace and harmony regardless of the judgment's outcome, underscoring their commitment to maintaining a tranquil atmosphere after the verdict in the Ayodhya case. This collective stance reflected a responsible and conciliatory approach within the Muslim community. Numerous Muslim leaders and prominent figures welcomed the Ayodhya verdict, displaying a spirit of unity and respect for the Supreme Court's decision. Among them, K.K. Muhammad, a former ASI official, expressed his satisfaction with the judgment, citing the reliance on ASI's report as a positive aspect. BJP leader Shazia Ilmi praised the balanced nature of the Supreme Court's decision and called for collective efforts towards India's progress. Iqbal Ansari, one of the litigants in the Ayodhya case, expressed his happiness with the verdict. Political leaders like Afzal Ansari of the Bahujan Samaj Party (BSP) welcomed the judgment, emphasizing the need for unity and brotherhood. Notably, Islamic scholars also endorsed the verdict. Governor of Kerala Arif Mohammad Khan urged everyone to respect and follow the Supreme Court's decision. Ajmer Dargah's spiritual leader, Zainul Abedin Ali Khan, called for harmony and peace, while Zufar Faruqi, chairman of the Uttar Pradesh Sunni Central Waqf Board, stated that he would not file any review or curative petition, thus showing acceptance for the Supreme Court's verdict. This collective acceptance of the judgment highlights a commitment to peace, unity and respect for the rule of law in India.

The historic verdict transcends the boundaries of mere land disputes and notions of winning or losing. It still stands as a powerful symbol of unity and harmony in a diverse nation like India. Lord Shri Ram, a deity who is revered and cherished by millions, belongs to everyone. His presence in the collective consciousness of the Indian people is a unifying force that bridges differences and fosters a sense of shared heritage. In this light, it becomes clear that no one truly loses in a verdict that upholds the principles of justice and equality.

Former President Ram Nath Kovind, captured this sentiment eloquently when he said, 'Sri Ram is of everyone. He is in everyone.'[33] This statement by him reinforces the idea that Lord Ram's significance goes beyond religious affiliations and encompasses the entire Indian populace. It serves as a call for unity and inclusivity, emphasizing that the spirit of Lord Ram resides within every Indian, regardless of their faith.

In essence, the Ayodhya Ram Janmabhoomi Temple judgment serves as a reminder of India's diverse yet harmonious story, where the legacy of Lord Shri Ram binds the nation together. It signifies a collective victory for the people of India, strengthening the bonds of unity and underscoring the enduring spirit of Bharat.

4

FROM VERDICT TO VISION

The verdict on Ayodhya and the subsequent initiation of the Ram temple construction represented a significant milestone in India's history, embodying the resolution of a prolonged socio-religious dispute and the fulfilment of a cherished aspiration for millions. As per the court's orders, the land awarded to Ram Lalla was to remain under the care of a statutory receiver until a board of trustees was instituted to oversee the temple's construction and administration.

On 5 February 2020, PM Narendra Modi revealed through his Twitter (now X) account the impending formation of the trust to supervise the construction of the temple, underlining that the government's plan of establishing the trust was aligned with the esteemed verdict of the Supreme Court of India.[1] During a session in the Lok Sabha, he announced the establishment of an independent 15-member trust. Prime Minister Modi's announcement was accompanied by his call for all parliamentarians to lend their support to the temple's construction, a call that garnered appreciation from politicians representing diverse viewpoints. Prime Minister Modi further commended the poised demeanour of citizens following the verdict and their resolute trust in democratic establishments. Home Minister Amit Shah, through his tweets, affirmed the autonomy of the trust and its composition of 15 members, including a representative from the Dalit community.

The establishment of the trust marks a significant chapter in the enduring saga of faith and devotion associated with Lord Ram and the sacred land of Ayodhya. To fully comprehend the significance of this monumental step, it is imperative to trace the journey of the Ram Janmabhoomi Nyas (RJN)—a precursor that symbolically set the stage for the Shri Ram Janmabhoomi Teertha Kshetra's inception.

THE ETERNAL THREAD: NYAS TO TEERTHA KSHETRA

In a significant stride, the RJN, also referred to as the Nyas, emerged as an autonomous trust on 25 January 1993, under the aegis of the VHP. Its inception was aimed at assuming custodianship of the Ram Janmabhoomi site and orchestrating the realization of the envisioned Ram temple. Mahant Ramchandra Das Paramhans (1913–2003) held the mantle of leadership, succeeded by Mahant Nritya Gopal Das after his demise. The underlying motive for its creation was to avert potential government control and interference in the temple's construction, thus preserving the RJN's autonomy. The RJN established operational workshops within Karsevakpuram, a prominent encampment of kar sevaks situated in Ayodhya, and readied itself for the temple's construction.

The RJN emerged as a steadfast proponent of the construction of a grand Ram temple in Ayodhya. This visionary trust assumed the responsibility of nurturing the collective aspirations of countless devotees who held the cherished belief that the site was the birthplace of Lord Shri Ram. The RJN embarked on a multifaceted journey, channelling its efforts towards advocating, planning and eventually overseeing the temple's construction.

Through awareness campaigns, public gatherings and tireless advocacy, it kindled a flame of devotion that burned brightly, even in the face of challenges and adversities. It played a pivotal role in land acquisition, facilitating a space that would serve as a canvas for the sacred architectural marvel to be etched on it in the future.

The Teertha Kshetra, borne from this legacy, stands as a testament to the power of collective faith, collaboration and unwavering determination.

SHRI RAM JANMABHOOMI TEERTHA KSHETRA: A NEW CHAPTER UNFOLDS

The Ram Janmabhoomi Teertha Kshetra is not merely a physical entity but a living embodiment of the ideals championed by the Nyas. It is a manifestation of the undying spirit that propelled the Nyas forward. And now, under the auspices of the Shri Ram Janmabhoomi Teertha Kshetra Trust, that spirit has only continued to guide the temple's journey. In this seamless transition from Nyas to Teertha Kshetra, a sacred torch has been passed, illuminating the path of devotion, unity and reverence, for generations to come.

The Trust

While making the announcement for the Trust in Lok Sabha, PM Narendra Modi had said that the Union Cabinet had decided to transfer 67.703 acres of land to the Trust. The Trust was entrusted with the responsibility of planning, designing and supervising the construction of the temple. Of the 15 trustees, 12 members were nominated by the government, and during the first meeting, an additional three members were selected. It was established that the nominated members of the Trust were required to be practising Hindus.[2]

The temple Trust was initially headed by Kesava Iyengar Parasaran as its acting president. Parasaran, referred to as 'God's advocate' is the 92-year-old senior lawyer who fought the Ram Janmabhoomi case in Supreme Court as the lead counsel for the Hindu parties. He successfully argued for the possession of the entire disputed land in favour of the deity 'Ram Lalla Virajman'.[3] He had also allowed his house in Delhi to be used as the Trust's office. The central government officially notified the Trust on 5 February 2020, designating its registered office at Parasaran's residence.[4]

The trustees gathered for their inaugural meeting on 19 February 2020. This laid the cornerstone for their ambitious mission. With this first meeting came the essential task of completing the ensemble of nominated members. Once united, the Trust embarked on an inspiring journey of shaping their vision into reality.

The nine permanent members include:

1. Shri K. Parasaran—the founding trustee and one of the senior-most advocates of the Supreme Court,

currently serving as the senior spokesperson of the trust

2. Jagatguru Shankaracharya Jyothish Peethadheswar Swami Vasudevanand Saraswati Ji Maharaj—a religious leader from Prayagraj

3. Jagatguru Madhavarcharya Swami Vishwa Prasannatheerth Ji Maharaj—a religious leader from Pejawar Math, Udupi

4. Yugpurusha Parmanand Giri Ji Maharaj—a religious leader from Haridwar

5. Swami Govind Dev Giri Ji Maharaj—a religious leader from Pune, who currently holds the position of the treasurer of the Trust

6. Mahant Dinendra Das Ji—a representative from the Nirmohi Akhara

7. Vimlendra Mohan Pratap Mishra—a descendant of Ayodhya's royal family representing the Ayodhya district

8. Dr Anil Mishra—a homeopathic doctor from Ayodhya as a representative of the Ayodhya district

9. Shri Kameshwar Chaupal—a representative from the Dalit community (Scheduled Caste) from Patna, the individual who laid the foundation stone of the Ram temple in 1989 during the 'shilanyas' event organized by the VHP

The six nominated members, as stipulated by the government, are to be as follows:

1. The Trust, in its first meeting, unanimously elected Mahant Nrityagopal Das Ji Maharaj as the president/chairman of the Trust. Nrityagopal Das is the head

of Ayodhya's largest temple, the Mani Ram Das Ki Chavani.[5]

2. Champat Rai, who is the vice-president of Vishva Hindu Parishad, was elected as the general secretary of the trust.

3. A representative nominated by the central government, who must be a serving member of the Indian Administrative Service, at least at the joint secretary level.

4. A representative nominated by the state government, serving as a member of the Indian Administrative Service under the state government.

5. District Magistrate, Ayodhya, to hold the position of an ex-officio trustee. In the event that the serving district magistrate is not a practicing Hindu, an additional magistrate to be appointed to the board.

6. The chairman responsible for the administration and development of the Ram temple complex to be chosen by the board of trustees, who would also serve as an ex-officio trustee. In the same meeting on 19 February, the third member to be nominated was Shri Nripendra Mishra, former IAS officer.[6] The trust formed a Nirman Samiti (Construction Committee), and its leadership was entrusted to Shri Mishra as its chairman.[7]

Among the 15 members, only 11 trustees hold voting rights. The two officers appointed by the state and central government, the district collector of Ayodhya and the representative of Nirmohi Akhara, do not possess voting rights during the Trust's proceedings.

In the course of the first meeting of the newly formed Trust, a total of nine resolutions were passed. Among these, one expressed gratitude to PM Narendra Modi, the central government and the UP government for their proactive involvement throughout the entire process. The trustees also honoured the memory of those who made supreme sacrifices for this noble cause. A resolution was passed to commemorate their dedication and sacrifice. Following the meeting, Mahant Nrityagopal Das affirmed his commitment to honour the sentiments of the people and expressed that the commencement of temple construction is imminent. He also conveyed that the core architectural blueprint of the Ram temple will closely mirror the vision put forth by the VHP.[8]

SAMARPAN DRIVE: THE PEOPLE'S CONTRIBUTION

In the tapestry of India's spiritual landscape, a deeply ingrained faith and belief in ideals weaves the essence of devotion. This tradition, exemplified by the restoration of the iconic Somnath Temple in Gujarat after the dawn of India's Independence, speaks to the soul of the nation. In the case of Somnath, Mahatma Gandhi advocated that the temple's revival should be a labour of love by the people, their financial contributions symbolizing the devotion that resides in the hearts of millions, entirely separate from government funding. As history unfurled, the reconstructed Somnath Temple stood as a testament to the ideals of faith, unity and public spirit. Today, this notion finds a symphony of resonance in the Ayodhya Ram temple's saga. Here, a similar *samarpan* (devotion) drive unites people in a spiritual symphony. The heart of both endeavours beats with the same rhythm—a rhythm of unwavering devotion and a chorus of collective commitment, all sustained solely by the contributions of the people.

Creating a bridge between the sacred and the tangible, a collaborative endeavour between the VHP, the RSS and the Shri Ram Janmabhoomi Teerth Kshetra Trust gave rise to an extensive donation campaign that was set to unfold over a period of one and a half months. Thus, the biggest crowdfunding drive of the world—the Shri Ram Janmabhoomi Mandir Nidhi Samarpan Abhiyan—was launched.

Initially, the estimated cost for constructing the magnificent Ram Temple in Ayodhya was approximated to be ₹1,800 crore.[9] The core essence of the Samarpan drive initiative was grounded in the unwavering belief that the temple is a devoted offering to Lord Ram, and any financial constraint would not hinder the progress of this divine undertaking. General Secretary Champat Rai too has said that the ambitious scope of this initiative was to traverse every corner of the country, from the northern reaches of Kashmir to the southern tip of Kanyakumari, from the western border to the eastern edge, leaving no stone unturned.[10] The objective was to not only disseminate information about the Ram Temple but also create a profound awareness among the masses while seeking their invaluable support. Commencing on the auspicious occasion of Makar Sankranti on 15 January 2021, this intensive and extensive campaign was meticulously designed to span until Magh Purnima which fell on 27 February 2021. The campaign was set to reach an astonishing 110 million families residing in 400,000 villages across the nation, guided by the dedicated efforts of VHP *karyakarta*s (workers).[11] In this collective endeavour, the Ram Temple transformed into more than just a place of worship; it took on the significance of a 'Rashtra Mandir'—a temple that symbolizes the nation itself. It provided a platform for individuals from all corners of the country to contribute to a shared dream that resonated deeply with millions—the construction of a temple at the birthplace of Bhagwan Shri Ram. The actual response was overwhelming, with donations pouring in from citizens, organizations and communities.[12]

The donation drive was initiated simultaneously from 400 different locations.[13] The VHP started its campaign with a donation of ₹500,100 from the first person of the country, President Ram Nath Kovind, on his and his family's behalf.[14] Vice President M. Venkaiah Naidu followed suit, along with several state governors and CMs who also made contributions for the temple construction.[15]

Within 11 months of it being set up, the Shri Ram Janmabhoomi Teertha Kshetra Trust managed to collect a little over ₹100 crore, with the Gujarat-based spiritual leader Morari Bapu contributing the highest donation of ₹11.3 crore, with his followers in the US, Canada and the UK having collected another ₹8 crore.[16] The funds received by the Trust through this campaign crossed ₹2,500 crore,[17] and the figure was expected to only go up.

As per Swami Govind Dev Giri, treasurer of the Trust, it was observed that contributions were made to the fundraising campaign by individuals across various communities and age groups. He mentioned that even children contributed from their piggy banks, while individuals with occupations such as labourers, beggars, vendors and rickshaw pullers donated according to their capacity. Swami ji stated that donations were received from all corners of the country encompassing people of different castes, creeds and religions.[18] Shri Ram Janmabhoomi Teerth Kshetra Trust on 6 March 2021 said through a tweet that Arunachal Pradesh had contributed ₹4.5 crore, Manipur ₹2 crore, Mizoram ₹21 lakh, Nagaland ₹28 lakh and Meghalaya ₹85 lakh for the purpose.[19] As informed by general secretary of the Trust, Champat Rai, Rajasthan made the highest contribution in the Samarpan Drive, with a collection of more than ₹500 crore.[20]

Amidst heartwarming instances of devotion and selflessness, the narrative of contributions towards the construction of the grand Ram Mandir in Ayodhya takes on a deeply moving dimension. In a striking testament to the power of faith over material circumstances, a 90-year-old woman, despite her financial limitations, made a donation to the Shri Ram Janmabhoomi Mandir Nidhi Samarpan Abhiyan.[21] Her gesture underscored the belief that the value of the contribution lies not in its monetary worth but in the love and devotion with which it is offered. Similarly, another elderly woman from Telangana, surviving on a meagre pension, donated ₹500 towards the temple's construction. When questioned about her decision, she expressed that her faith in Bhagwan Ram's providence was her source of reassurance, stating that her devotion outweighed her concerns about her pension-dependent livelihood. Take the case of Munnibai Khushwaha, a resident of Madhya Pradesh's Vidisha. She ekes out a living by selling plums. However, her modest means did not deter her from contributing to the grand vision of the Shri Ram Mandir.[22] With a heart full of devotion, she contributed coins, ₹10 and ₹20 notes, totaling ₹100. Welcoming the volunteers with open arms, she offered them tea and plums, while sharing her belief that Bhagwan Shri Ram's blessings transcend distinctions of wealth, age and gender. Her conviction showcased the unifying power of devotion.

Individuals across India viewed the construction of the Ram Temple not merely as a religious undertaking but as a national project. Zahara Begum, based in Andhra Pradesh and the organizer of the Tahera Trust operating in Telangana and Andhra Pradesh, called on to the Muslim community to contribute to the Ram Temple construction in Ayodhya. This call has resonated with many Muslim families in villages, inspiring them to come forward and contribute. Begum, who is currently in the USA, emphasized that this gesture is a way of reciprocating the goodwill extended by Hindu communities in villages, who have helped the Muslim community by donating land for mosques and other religious structures.[23] Another example is that of Wasim Rizvi, former chairman of Uttar Pradesh Shia Central Waqf Board, who publicly announced his contribution of ₹51,000 towards the construction of the Ram Temple in Ayodhya.

The contributions received from across regions and religions not only reflected the importance of the temple for many but also showcased the unity and solidarity of the Indian populace. 'Donors' devotion is so deep that they continued sending money to our accounts even when the pandemic had brought the entire country to a standstill,' Prakash Gupta, an RSS member who runs the Trust's office, told reporters in Ayodhya.[24] In a press release, the VHP stated that the campaign had captured indelible, astonishing and heartwarming moments.

The donation drive was, thus, underpinned by a robust organizational structure. The trust ensured utmost transparency in its financial operations by issuing printed coupons and receipts of denominations such as ₹10, ₹100 and ₹1000.[25] The trust's transparent handling of funds lent credibility and trustworthiness to the campaign. This sense of assurance encouraged individuals from all walks of life to contribute to a cause that had transcended mere religious boundaries. The campaign's success was also attributed to the outreach strategy. The drive's organizers, including the VHP, employed various mediums to reach out to people, from door-to-door interactions to social media campaigns. This comprehensive approach ensured that no corner of the nation remained untouched, making the drive accessible to every willing participant.

FOUNDATION OF FAITH: AYODHYA'S HISTORIC BHOOMI PUJAN

On the historic date of 5 August 2020, amidst the ancient city of Ayodhya, a resounding echo of devotion and aspiration reverberated in the air. In a convergence of faith, tradition and monumental significance, the auspicious occasion of Ayodhya Ram Temple *bhoomi pujan* (ceremony for offering reverence to Mother Earth) announced the starting of a new chapter in India's civilizational heritage.

Even before the Supreme Court's verdict in November 2019, substantial efforts had been underway for constructing the Ram Temple. In the 1980s, the VHP had initiated fundraising campaigns and had amassed funds and bricks inscribed with the slogan 'Jai Shri Ram'. The then Rajiv Gandhi government had officially authorized the VHP to conduct the shilanyas. This permission had been conveyed to VHP leader Ashok

Singhal by the home minister of that time. Although there had been an initial agreement to hold the shilanyas ceremony away from the disputed site, a faction of VHP leaders and sadhus had commenced the ceremony adjacent to the contested land on 9 November 1989. This location eventually became the main entrance (Singhdwar) of the sanctum.

Following the Supreme Court judgment in November 2019, preliminary work at the Ram Temple site by the Trust commenced in March 2020. Remarkable findings emerged during the ground-levelling and excavation process, including intricate carvings on sandstone, a shivalinga, pillars and fragments of idols.[26] Lord Ram's idol was carefully relocated to a temporary site in March 2020. However, in 2020, work at the site faced temporary disruptions due to the Covid-19 pandemic and Indo-China border tensions.

The symbolic construction officially commenced after the grand bhoomi pujan ceremony. Dignitaries, including the PM, religious leaders, political figures and devotees, attended the event.[27] Prime Minisiter Modi shared the dais with four other people—Mohan Bhagwat, RSS chief; Nritya Gopal Das Maharaj, Trust chief; Anandiben Patel, UP Governor; and Yogi Adityanath, UP CM.[28] The first invitation for the event was extended to Iqbal Ansari, a prominent Muslim litigant in the Ayodhya dispute. A diverse guest list included approximately 50 saints hailing from different corners of India. Notable names gracing the occasion encompassed Faizabad MP Lallu Singh; BJP national president, JP Nadda; deputy CMs of UP, Dinesh Sharma and Keshav Prasad Maurya; BJP leader Vinay Katiyar; former Madhya Pradesh CM Uma Bharti; Swami Narendra Giri of

Akhada Parishad, Sadhvi Ritambhara; spiritual leader Sri Sri
Ravi Shankar; and yog guru Ramdev. Hindu seers including
Mahant Ram Tapeshawar Das of Janaki Mandir, Janakapur,
Nepal; and Mahant Jagganath Das of Matihani Temple, Nepal
were also graciously invited. Janakpur shares connections
with Uttar Pradesh Bihar and Ayodhya. Additionally, Sikh
jathedars and priests, along with the chairman of the Sunni
Waqf Board from Lucknow and several other religious
leaders joined the historic event. Padma Shri recipient
Mohammad Sharif, known for his selfless act of cremating
over 10,000 unclaimed bodies, was among the invitees.
Considering the ongoing pandemic, the seating arrangements
were meticulously organized to adhere to social distancing
guidelines, ensuring the safety and well-being of all attendees.
Salil Singhal, nephew of VHP leader Ashok Singhal, was the
mukhya yajman (chief guest) of the bhoomi pujan ceremony
along with his wife.

   In Ayodhya, PM Modi's visit commenced with a warm
welcome from UP CM Yogi Adityanath. Their first stop was
the historic tenth-century Hanumangarhi temple, where they
came together to offer prayers to Lord Hanuman.[29] During
this visit, PM Modi received several symbolic gifts, including
a traditional headgear, a silver crown and a stole bearing the
name of Lord Ram. After their visit to the Hanumangarhi
temple, the delegation proceeded to the Ram Janmabhoomi
site. There, PM Modi paid his respects to Ram Lalla and
participated in the laying of the foundation stone for the
upcoming Shri Ram temple. As a symbolic gesture, he also
planted a *parijat* sapling,[30] a revered and divine plant, just
ahead of the foundation stone-laying ceremony for the temple.

   During the bhoomi pujan, rituals and prayers were

performed to seek divine blessings and ensure the successful and auspicious commencement of the construction work. The bhoomi and *shila* pujan ceremonies included chanting of mantras, shovelling of earth and worship of the ground and shila. The event precisely occurred during a specified period of thirty-two seconds—*abhijit muhurta*—at 12.15 p.m.,[31] the most auspicious moment for the foundation-stone laying of the temple, according to the well-known astrologer Acharya Ganeshwar Raj Rajeshwar Shastri Dravid of Kashi, Varanasi.[32] Prime Minister Modi himself brought a silver *kalash* (urn) and placed it in the designated place.[33] Nine bricks[34] were laid down in the sanctum sanctorum to mark the beginning of the construction process. The priest explained the significance of these nine bricks during the bhoomi pujan. He also mentioned that there were 2,75,000[35] such bricks that were sent by devotees of Lord Ram from around the world in 1989, out of which 100 bricks with 'Jai Shri Ram'[36] engraving had been taken for this purpose, out of which nine were used for the bhoomi pujan. Soil and water from Sangam[37]—the confluence of the Ganga, Yamuna and Saraswati rivers—was carried to Ayodhya for the bhoomi pujan. Soil from more than 2,000 pilgrimage sites and water from 100 sacred rivers were brought to be used for purification and other rituals during this ceremony.[38] Prime Minister Modi unveiled a plaque as rememberance of the ceremony and released a commemorative postage stamp on Shri Ram Janmabhoomi Mandir. The entire event was broadcasted live on Doordarshan, the national broadcasting network, enabling all Indians to virtually attend the ceremony and witness the laying of the foundation stone, bringing the realization of a national dream one step closer.

After the ceremony, CM Yogi Adityanath addressed the gathering and emphasized that the temple's construction would not only amplify Ayodhya's splendour but also bring about a transformative effect on the region's economy. He envisioned new opportunities and a global influx of visitors who would come to pay their respects to Lord Ram and Goddess Sita, catalysing a radical transformation.

Referring to the diverse unity that the temple signifies, PM Modi highlighted the global resonance of the event. He emphasized that people from various countries celebrate this harmonious blend of cultures and faiths, paying homage to Lord Ram. In his address, PM Modi said, 'The time has come when a proper temple can be provided to the deity of Lord Ram by moving it from the make-shift tent and canopy, where it was kept for decades. A grand temple will now be built for our Lord Ram. Today, the Ram Janmabhoomi has become free from the centuries-old chain of destruction and resurrection.'[39]

Prime Minister Modi compared the struggles and sacrifices made for the Ram Temple to those made during the Indian freedom struggle. He further added:

> Several generations devoted themselves completely during our freedom struggle. There was never a moment during the period of slavery that there was not a movement for freedom. There was not a place in our country where sacrifices were not made for the freedom. 15th August is the embodiment of sacrifices of the lakhs of people and a deep yearning for the independence. Similarly, several generations have made self-less sacrifices for several centuries for the

construction of the Ram Temple. Today marks the culmination of that centuries-old penance, sacrifices and resolve. There was sacrifice, dedication and resolve during the movement for the construction of the Ram Temple and that dream is being realized today because of their sacrifices and struggle. I, on behalf of the 130 crore people of the country, salute them and bow before them for their sacrifices which have led to the foundation of the Ram Temple.[40]

Prime Minister Modi said that the Ram Temple would be the modern symbol of our culture. It will symbolize our eternal hope. Concluding his address, he said:

Rama speaks, thinks and acts according to time, place and circumstances. Lord Ram teaches us how to grow and move with time. Lord Ram is the advocate of change and modernity. India is moving ahead today profoundly with these inspirations, these ideals of Lord Ram. Lord Ram has taught us how to fulfil our duties. He also taught us how to face challenges and how to seek and attain knowledge. The Ram Mandir should be built with bricks of love, respect and brotherhood.[41]

Entwined with the bhoomi pujan ceremony, PM Narendra Modi's presence etched a new chapter in India's contemporary narrative. A global summon had been beckoned by the Trust from the heart of Ayodhya to the devout worldwide. Respected saints, mahatmas and followers of Lord Ram had been urged to unite in a harmonious symphony of prayers and *bhajan-kirtan*. Between 11.30 a.m. and 12.30 p.m., families, friends and communities encouraged each other to participate in

shared devotion. Virtual halls resonated with the chorus;
adorned homes, temples and local markets were enveloped
in prasad-laden celebration. As twilight descended, the warm
glow of innumerable diyas signified collective reverence. In
the countdown to 5 August, a ritual of consecration had
drawn close. Soil and water culled from revered landmarks,
from the hallowed Shri Badrinath Dham to the formidable
Raigad Fort, from the sacred Ranganathswami Mandir to the
venerable Shri Mahakaleshwar Mandir, from the birthplaces
of illustrious souls like Hutatma Chandra Shekhar Azad and
Bhagwan Birsa Munda—all had converged on Ayodhya's
embrace. A mosaic of pious elements, woven with the threads
of faith and nationalism, had arrived to bless the grounds of
Ayodhya Dham. Amidst the sacredness of the bhoomi pujan,
the foundation stone of the temple was laid, marking the
formal commencement of the project.

Various individuals and temples across different regions
also participated in symbolic religious actions to mark the
occasion of the bhoomi pujan. The illumination of earthen
lamps in the premises of temples, such as Badrinath and
Gopinath temples in Uttarakhand's Chamoli, Mata Mansa Devi
temple in Haryana's Panchkula and Mahakaleshwar Temple in
Madhya Pradesh's Ujjain, illustrates the collective celebration
and reverence for the bhoomi pujan across different parts of
India. Indian–Americans in the US celebrated the ceremony
by lighting diyas and displaying digital images of the Ram
Temple on a tableau truck near Capitol Hill. Later in the
day, after the bhoomi pujan ceremony, a Ram Mandir digital
billboard came up in New York's Times Square.[42]

The diverse ways in which individuals and communities
commemorated and participated underscored the emotional

and spiritual significance attached to the construction of the Ram Mandir in Ayodhya. L.K. Advani, who had transformed a local legal dispute into a national movement for the Ram Temple's construction, expressed that destiny had led him to play a pivotal role through the Ram Rath Yatra. Calling 5 August as a historic and emotional day, he highlighted that significant dreams take time to realize, but when they do, the wait becomes worthwhile.[43] Congress leader Rahul Gandhi tweeted in Hindi, asserting that Lord Ram represents supreme human values such as love, compassion and justice.[44] He stated that Ram embodies these values and cannot be associated with hatred, cruelty or injustice. RSS chief, Mohan Bhagwat, acknowledged the sacrifices made during the struggle for the Ram Temple and noted that many people could not be present physically due to the pandemic but were present in spirit.

The ceremony was a cause for widespread celebration and elation among almost all politicians and the general populace. Yet, a few expressed concerns questioning the PM's presence at the bhoomi pujan. These concerns find historical context in similar instances where political figures participated in temple inaugurations. The episode involving PM Indira Gandhi's inauguration of the Bharat Mata Mandir in Haridwar in 1983 is intriguing.[45] Another such instance was of the inauguration of the Somnath Temple. At that time, PM Nehru expressed reservations about President Prasad's presence, citing his vision of a secular India. President Prasad's stance, however, highlighted the importance of fostering interfaith harmony, emphasizing that rebuilding the temple aimed to provide every caste and community with a sense of unity and freedom. In light of these historical parallels,

PM Modi's participation in the puja stands as a testament to India's rich tapestry of faith, unity and cultural diversity. India's stance on secularism has transcended Jawaharlal Nehru's belief in the strict separation of religion and state. Today's leaders continue to honour the nation's collective heritage while upholding its commitment to secularism and inclusivity. Moreover, our secularism acknowledges the coexistence of various faiths within a diverse cultural fabric.

THE SACRED LAND: ACQUISITION AND SYMBOLISM

Amidst the sacred echoes of Ayodhya, where history, faith and devotion intertwine, the land is not merely measured in square feet, it is enriched with the aspirations of millions, now becoming the canvas for a symbol of unity and reverence—the Ram Temple. With each acre acquired for the construction of this temple, a story of dedication and determination is etched into the very soil that will cradle this magnificent edifice. As the Shri Ram Janmabhoomi Teerth Kshetra embraces these parcels, it isn't just the land that changes hands, it's a transformation of sentiments into architecture, and of a timeless journey that has brought a nation together.

Following the Supreme Court judgment, PM Narendra Modi declared the allocation of 67.703 acres of land to the Trust, with the aim of upholding the sanctity of Ayodhya and facilitating the construction of the Ram temple.[46] These 67 acres, adjoining the disputed 2.77 acres, were the same ones acquired by the government in 1993 through The Acquisition of Certain Area at Ayodhya Act.

During the initial week of March 2021, the Trust made

A grateful acceptance by PM: The pran pratishtha of Shri Vigraha of Bhagwan Shri Ram Lalla Sarkar will be performed by PM Narendra Modi in Shri Ram Janmabhoomi Mandir on 22 January 2024.

Photo Courtesy: Official Twitter account of Shri Ram Janmabhoomi Teerth Kshetra (@ShriRamTeerth) dated 25 October 2023

Shila pujan by CM Yogi Adityanath: Laying the foundation stone for mandir's garbha griha

Photo Courtesy: Official Twitter account of Shri Ram Janmabhoomi Teerth Kshetra (@ShriRamTeerth) dated 1 June 2022

Divya darshan (sacred viewing) of Bhagwan Shri Ram Lalla Virajman on the sacred occasion of Ram Mandir's bhoomi pujan on 5 August 2020

Photo Courtesy: Official Twitter account of Shri Ram Janmabhoomi Teerth Kshetra (@ShriRamTeerth) dated 5 August 2020

Rising with devotion: Building the first floor of the temple structure

Photo Courtesy: Official Twitter account of Shri Ram Janmabhoomi Teerth Kshetra (@ShriRamTeerth) dated 8 July 2023

Men at work: Carefully crafted stones that will stick together, brick by brick, to make way for Ram's abode

Photo Courtesy: Official Twitter account of Shri Ram Janmabhoomi Teerth Kshetra (@ShriRamTeerth) dated 9 October 2023

Gateway to devotion: Frame of the Ram Janmabhoomi Singh Dwar

Photo Courtesy: Official Twitter account of Shri Ram Janmabhoomi Teerth Kshetra (@ShriRamTeerth) dated 9 October 2023

Resurrecting history: The pillars, idols and shivalinga unearthed at Shri Ram Janmabhoomi

Photo Courtesy: Official Twitter account of Shri Ram Janmabhoomi Teerth Kshetra (@ShriRamTeerth) dated 12 September 2023

Divine blueprint: The Kali Yuga abode of the Treta deity

Photo Courtesy: Official Twitter account of Shri Ram Janmabhoomi Teerth Kshetra (@ShriRamTeerth) dated 15 October 2022

A diagonal view of faith: The temple model from another perspective

Photo Courtesy: Official Twitter account of Shri Ram Janmabhoomi Teerth Kshetra (@ShriRamTeerth) dated 15 October 2022

The transformation from vision to reality: Faithfully mirroring the design

Photo Courtesy: Official Twitter account of Shri Ram Janmabhoomi Teerth Kshetra (@ShriRamTeerth) dated 16 October 2023

Shri Ram Mandir Construction Committee holds on-site inspection with Nripendra Mishra.

Photo Courtesy: Official Twitter account of Shri Ram Janmabhoomi Teerth Kshetra (@ShriRamTeerth) dated 17 December 2022

A bow to Ram Lalla: Prime Minister Modi's spiritual visit in 2022 for Deepotsav celebration in Ayodhya

Photo Courtesy: Official Twitter account of Shri Ram Janmabhoomi Teerth Kshetra (@ShriRamTeerth) dated 23 October 2022

A divine confluence of faith and governance: PM Modi and CM Yogi oversee ongoing construction at Ram Janmasthan

Photo Courtesy: Official Twitter account of Shri Ram Janmabhoomi Teerth Kshetra (@ShriRamTeerth) dated 24 October 2022

President Kovind's reverence: Cultivating faith by planting the seeds of devotion at Ayodhya's sacred ground

Photo Courtesy: Official Twitter account of Shri Ram Janmabhoomi Teerth Kshetra (@ShriRamTeerth) dated 29 August 2021

An auspicious occasion: PM Modi performs the bhoomi pujan ceremony on 5 August 2020

Photo Courtesy: Official Twitter account of Shri Ram Janmabhoomi Teerth Kshetra (@ShriRamTeerth) dated 5 August 2020

PM Modi and CM Yogi in the bhoomi pujan ceremony: Spearheading Ayodhya's unprecedented transformation

Photo Courtesy: Official Twitter account of Shri Ram Janmabhoomi Teerth Kshetra (@ShriRamTeerth) dated 5 August 2020

Intricately crafted: The exquisite roof of Shri Ram Mandir's garbha griha

Photo Courtesy: Official Twitter account of Shri Champat Rai (@ChampatRaiVHP) dated 12 August 2023

Building faith brick by brick: The divine realm amidst the radiant sun

Photo Courtesy: Official Twitter account of Shri Champat Rai (@ChampatRaiVHP) dated 16 May 2023

A grand vision unfolding: The majestic Ram Mandir takes shape.

Photo Courtesy: Official Twitter account of Shri Champat Rai (@ChampatRaiVHP) dated 16 October 2023

Ground floor triumph: A view from above

Photo Courtesy: Official Twitter account of Shri Champat Rai (@ChampatRaiVHP) dated 20 August 2023

Rising to the skies: Aerial view of Ram Mandir construction

Photo Courtesy: Official Twitter account of Shri Champat Rai (@ChampatRaiVHP) dated 22 April 2023

Glistening in the divine sunlight: Sculpted beauty at Ram Temple construction

Photo Courtesy: Official Twitter account of Shri Champat Rai (@ChampatRaiVHP) dated 23 May 2023

Crafting timeless devotion: Artistry on temple pillars

Photo Courtesy: Official Twitter account of Shri Champat Rai (@ChampatRaiVHP) dated 26 July 2023

Unearthed treasures: The land levelling at Ram Janmabhoomi in May 2020 uncovered several works of art including a 5-ft shivalinga, seven black touchstone pillars, six red sandstone pillars and broken idols of deities.

Photo Courtesy: Official Twitter account of Shri Champat Rai (@ChampatRaiVHP) dated 13 September 2023 an additional land acquisition by procuring 676.85 sq. ft of land adjacent to the 70-acre Ram Janmabhoomi premises. The land was secured from Swami Deepnarayan for ₹1 crore[47]. This newly acquired tract of land is strategically located next to the renowned Asharfi Bhawan. Towards the second half of March, the Trust acquired approximately 1.15 lakh sq. ft of land located around 2–3 km away from the Ram Janmabhoomi premises.[48] This acquisition is aimed to develop facilities for security forces, devotees and various activities related to the Trust's initiatives. Two parcels of land are located in the Ram Kot and Tehri Bazaar localities.[49]

In July 2021, the Trust acquired approximately 4,514 sq. m of adjoining land to the Ram Temple complex.[50] This land includes the sites of several ancient temples, including Kaushalya Bhawan, Fikerah Ram Mandir and Deen Kuti Mandir, which have stood for 250 to 300 years. These temples share boundaries with the Ram Janmabhoomi campus. The owners of Kaushalya Bhawan, Mahant Kaushal Kishore Tripathi and Mahant Yashoda Nandan Tripathi were paid ₹4 crore and an alternative plot for their 1,881 sq. m of land. Similarly, Mahant Raghuvar Saran of Fikerah Ram Mandir received ₹3.70 crore and an alternate land for his 2,633 sq. m of temple land. The Trust also acquired Deen Kuti Mandir for ₹30 lakh from Mahant Sant Das. The Trust has also given its consent to demolishing nine temples on the Ram Janmabhoomi campus. Deities from these temples are planned to be relocated to a new temple.[51]

The decision to acquire neighbouring lands and older structures along the boundary of the temple complex aligns with the Trust's overarching strategy for expansion, consistent with the approved design for the grand temple. The objective of this expansion is to establish a cohesive boundary for the temple complex that would also accommodate various ancillary structures including a museum, library, *yajnashala* (hall for fire ritual) and a picture gallery depicting diverse episodes from Lord Ram's life.

Champat Rai emphasized that the whole process of acquiring the land is being conducted with utmost transparency. The acquisitions were executed in a manner consistent with the principles of openness and integrity. All the land procured was secured at rates significantly below prevailing market rates, showcasing the Trust's responsible approach to resource management.[52] Thus, the acquisition of additional land is part of the Trust's ongoing efforts to expand the Ram Janmabhoomi Temple complex and accommodate the various structures planned within the premises. The Trust's leadership had already pinpointed lands and properties within the Ramkot area that were earmarked for acquisition as part of the temple complex expansion. They initiated discussions with the respective owners to move forward with the process. And so, each piece of land acquired has been interweaving the threads of determination, faith and progress. The once-disputed stretch of land now stands united under the aegis of the Ram Temple, a testament to the power of a collective vision, perseverance and endeavour.

THE DIVINE BLUEPRINT: DESIGN, ARCHITECTURE AND PARTNERSHIPS

The architect entrusted with the intricate design of the Ram Temple in Ayodhya is Chandrakant Sompura. The Trust opted to retain his original plan for the Ram Temple that he created in 1988. Renowned for his architectural prowess, Chandrakant Sompura hails from a distinguished lineage of temple designers. Notably, his grandfather, Prabhakarji Sompura, played a pivotal role in conceiving the iconic Somnath Temple. The family's accomplishments encompass an extensive collection of temples, among them the Swaminarayan Mandir in Mumbai and the Birla Mandir in Kolkata.[53] Carrying forward this revered heritage, Chandrakant Sompura, in collaboration with his sons Nikhil and Ashish Sompura, has painstakingly crafted the blueprint of the Ram Temple.

Chandrakant Sompura's connection with the late VHP chief Ashok Singhal, was established through the Birla family, who had previously commissioned the design of the Birla Mandir in Kolkata. Back in the day, he used to visit Ayodhya to assess the land. Due to heightened security, he had to adopt the guise of a devotee, using footsteps to measure the area and create the masterplan. The design he had crafted had garnered approval from the sants and gurus during the Allahabad Kumbh in the early 1990s.[54] However, for the grand Ram Temple which is being built in the twenty-first century, the Sompuras have upgraded the original plan in keeping with the scale of the project. They submitted the new plan in July 2020, which was almost double the size of the original one.[55] Nikhil Sompura and Ashish Sompura drew the modified design of the temple.[56] However, the basic design has not been changed, according to Mahant Kamal Nayan Das, heir apparent of Mahant Nritya Gopal Das, chairman of the temple trust.[57]

THE ARCHITECTURAL SPLENDOUR: EXPLORING THE DESIGN ELEMENTS OF THE TEMPLE

For the construction of the Ram Temple, the process of land acquisition went beyond the allotted area, as already discussed in previous sections. According to the final blueprint, six temples of different deities are being constructed in the Ram Janmabhoomi premises. The temple complex thus encompasses a series of dedicated shrines, venerating an array of revered deities including Lord Surya, Lord Ganesha, Lord Shiva, Goddess Durga, Lord Vishnu and Lord Brahma. At the heart of this divine enclave stands the main temple, an architectural marvel that spans a sprawling area of 10 acres, while the remaining 57 acres have been planned to be developed as the temple complex. Its total built-up expanse extends over 57,400 sq. ft, while its impressive dimensions unfold with a length of 360 ft and a width of 235 ft. Ascending into the heavens, the temple reaches an awe-inspiring total height of 161 ft, inclusive of its majestic pinnacle. Comprising three floors, each boasting a height of 20 ft, the temple's structural integrity rests upon a remarkable assembly of 160 columns on the ground floor, 132 columns on the first floor and 74 columns on the second floor.[58] Amidst this architectural grandeur, the temple is adorned with five ornate pediments and pavilions, adding to its resplendent allure. Further enhancing its grand entrance are twelve elegantly designed gates, inviting devotees into a realm of spiritual devotion.[59]

The Trust released some photos of the proposed model for the Ram Mandir on its Twitter (now X) handle on 4 August 2020.[60] The Nagara style, typical of North Indian temples, is being employed, featuring an octagonal (*ashtabhuji*) structure. The temple's sanctum is octagonal in shape, while its structural perimeter forms a circular design, adhering to *vastu shastra* and *shilpa shastra* principles. The foundation of the temple has been formed using over two lakh bricks with 'Shri Ram' inscribed on them in various languages, collected over thirty years from across the country. The entrance on the east has been built in the Gopuram style, which represents the temples of the South. The walls of the temple display artworks depicting the life of Lord Shri Ram.[61]

Keeping in mind the area and aesthetic sense, the original design was altered to include three storeys and five *mandap*s (pavilion). The mandir has five domes and one tower with a height of 161 ft. The dome dimensions of the five mandaps measure 34 ft in width and 32 ft in length, with heights varying between 69 ft and 111 ft.[62] The three-tiered temple is designed with a central chamber, the sanctum sanctorum known as garbha griha. This architectural marvel is crafted to embrace the divine touch of sunlight gracing the idol of Ram Lalla, the divine embodiment in infancy. In the earlier design, there were two mandaps; three more have been added. Like the sanctorum, the Griha Mandap is fully covered, while the Keertan Mandap, the Nritya Mandap, the Rang Mandap and the two Prarthana Mandaps on each side are open areas.[63] Although the Nritya Mandap and Rang Mandap are part of ancient temple designs which were used as dancing mandaps, the plan now is to use that space for people to have darshan of Ram Lalla from three sides. Six more smaller temples will surround the main structure. The total area of the temple including the peripheral *parkota* (walled corridor) is 8.64 acres. The parkota is 762 m in length, with provision for these six temples and the facility of parikrama by devotees.[64]

The temple will feature 3,600 statues, each meticulously crafted based on Hindu *shastras* (scriptures). They will later be installed on pillars, bases and other designated places in the temple as per the construction schedule. The three-storied temple will also boast of a gold-studded door for the sanctum sanctorum, where the idol of five-ft-tall Ram Lalla statue will be put up on a platform.

According to an official statement, a total of 162 pillars have been completed, each meticulously crafted to bear the weight of more than 4,500 idols.[65] The process involves a systematic division of each pillar into three distinct sections. The upper part accommodates the carving of eight to twelve idols, the middle section encompasses four to eight, and the lower portion features four to six idols. These idols are being intricately carved onto the pillars, providing a visual depiction reminiscent of the Treta Yuga. The endeavour involves the collaborative efforts of 40 skilled artisans hailing from Kerala and Rajasthan, who have dedicated themselves to this artful task. The endeavor of carving a statue on each pillar requires the devoted craftsmanship of an artisan for approximately 200 days.

The temple is to be equipped with comprehensive lighting facilities, including ground uplighters, cove lighting, spot lighting and adaptable linear lighting.[66] Alongside, the lower plinth of the temple will serve as a canvas for the 3D portrayal of the legendary tales associated with Lord Ram, offering an immersive experience for visitors. Additionally, grand statues of Sita, Laxman, Hanuman and other significant deities from the Ramayana will grace the temple premises, contributing to its spiritual ambience.

The architectural framework of the Ram Mandir has been crafted from the exquisite Rajasthan Bansi Paharpur stone. A substantial quantity of approximately 4 lakh sq. ft of this unique pink marble stone is anticipated to be employed. Hailing from the Bayana Tehsil of Bharatpur District in Rajasthan, the Bansi Paharpur sandstone showcases captivating shades of pink and red. The remarkable Bansi Pahadpur sandstone has adorned numerous prestigious edifices across the nation, including the Akshardham Temple, the old Parliament complex and the iconic Lal Quila of Agra. The construction of the Ram Mandir stands resolute in utilizing this unparalleled stone, with a deliberate exclusion of steel or bricks in its structural makeup.

For the crafting of windows and doors, the material of choice is teak wood (*sagwan*), sourced from Maharashtra's Chandrapur region. The temple will have 46 doors made of teak wood. Teak wood, distinguished by its exceptional quality, boasts a remarkable lifespan exceeding a hundred years, making it an extraordinary choice for this purpose. The sanctum sanctorum, designated to house the revered idol of Ram Lalla, is undergoing meticulous carving with Makrana marble, encompassing pillars, beams, ceiling and wall cladding. Spanning an expansive area of 403.34 sq. ft, the sanctum sanctorum is said to boast dimensions of 20 ft in length and width.[67] To ensure structural integrity amidst various loads and climatic conditions, a total of 392 pillars have been strategically incorporated, aligning with the temple authorities' engineering considerations.[68]

SCULPTING THE IDOL OF RAM LALLA: THE SOUL OF THE SANCTUM

The central figure presiding over the temple is Ram Lalla Virajman, the infant incarnation of Lord Ram, a revered avatar of Lord Vishnu. Notably, Ram Lalla played a pivotal role in the protracted court case over the disputed site since 1989, earning recognition as a 'juristic person' under the law. Represented by Triloki Nath Pandey, a VHP leader, Ram Lalla found his voice and presence in the legal proceedings through his 'human' advocate.

The representation of Ram Lalla in his infant form holds profound significance in the context of the Ram Temple. This form represents purity, innocence and the potential for greatness, serving as a reminder of the divine purpose he fulfils in his life's journey. Devotees find solace and inspiration in worshiping the infant Lord, connecting with the idea that divinity and virtuous attributes are innate and transcend the boundaries of age and time. The deity will be worshipped in his child form at the Ram Janmabhoomi Temple.

As the sun transitions into *Makar Rashi* (astrological house of Capricorn) in 2024, Lord Ram will graciously occupy his revered seat within the temple's original sanctum sanctorum. The essence of Lord Ram will resonate in the temple through two magnificent idols. The first is a relic discovered in 1949 that has silently graced a humble tent for decades, the sanctity of its antiquity intact. The second idol—the main deity—will be the taller statue of Ram Lalla which would be visible to a devotee in the temple premises even from afar. The first idol will be respectfully relocated to a consecrated spot and hence will be the '*chal murti* (movable statue)'. Simultaneously, the second idol will ascend to the golden throne of the garbha griha. This idol would be chosen from the three idols that are being sculpted by three sculptors from three different stones separately. This chosen idol will permanently reside in the sanctum sanctorum, embodying the enduring spiritual essence of the deity.

It was Champat Rai who revealed that three master artisans are sculpting the Ram Lalla idol at three distinct corners of the sacred land of Ayodhya.[69] Ganesh Bhatt and his devoted disciple, Vipin Bhadoria, have been breathing life into Karnataka's stone. Simultaneously, Satya Narayan Pandey and his kin from Jaipur have summoned the grace of an 'A-class' Makrana stone, sculpting a masterpiece that echoes through the ages. In harmony, Arun Yogiraj, another luminary from Karnataka, is also shaping a unique vision in stone. These artisans, like custodians of a divine secret, mould not just stone but the very soul of Lord Ram. The idols emerge as silent narrators, whispering tales of devotion, craftsmanship and the timeless connection between the divine and the earthly realm.

The choice of the main deity among the three idols for the sanctum sanctorum on the ground floor would be taken once the idols are ready in their stones. Out of the remaning two idols, the second idol will find its place on the first floor, while the third one is destined for the second floor, where a dedicated space for Ram Darbar will be arranged.[70]

The construction of the sanctum sanctorum of the Ram Temple had been readied by August 2023 as the consecration of Ram Lalla is planned to take place in January 2024. A magnificent *pran pratishtha* or consecration ceremony, marking the installation of the deity, is scheduled to take place at the Ram Temple on 22 January 2024.[71] An elaborate affair, the ceremony is anticipated to draw a turnout of more than 5 million devotees in the first 50–60 days. The event is poised to be a multi-day spectacle, capturing the fervour and devotion of thousands who will gather to partake in this significant ceremony.

THE TEAM: COLLABORATIVE ENDEAVOURS AND EXPERT MANAGEMENT

November 2020 brought the guardians of the vision together, as the Trust convened in the Teen Murti Bhavan in New Delhi. Within this gathering, the Trust adorned the construction committee mantle in alignment with its foundational trust deed, fostering a unified spirit towards the temple's noble realization, as reported on the Trust's website. The Shri Ram Janmabhoomi Teerth Kshetra beckoned creative minds to contribute to the masterplan's embodiment. An open call resounded, seeking pro bono suggestions that would infuse the expansive canvas of the 70-acre Shri Ram Janmabhoomi Temple complex with dharmic yatra, rituals, culture and science. The call appeared as an invitation to breathe life into the temple's design and essence.[72]

The next month of the same year dawned with steadfast progress and thoughtful engagement. A heartfelt communication from Champat Rai encapsulated a snapshot of the ongoing endeavours in Ayodhya—an agreement inked with Larsen & Toubro (L&T) for building the main structure while Tata Consultancy Engineers Ltd (TCE) would develop the allied facilities. L&T volunteered to manage both the design and construction of the temple free of cost, holding the position of the project's contractor. Collaborating seamlessly, institutions like the Central Building Research Institute (CBRI), National Geophysical Research Institute and the prestigious Indian Institutes of Technology (Bombay, Guwahati and Madras) provided invaluable support in crucial domains like soil analysis, concrete work and architectural design. Additionally, TCE assumed the role of project management consultant, contributing their expertise to this monumental endeavour.[73]

VHP vice president Champat Rai revealed that L&T had put forth a proposal to construct the Ram Temple a decade ago, before the term of the then VHP working president, Ashok Singhal. Following the verdict of the Supreme Court, L&T reiterated its interest in the project, citing its possession of the requisite infrastructure and technical expertise for a project of such magnitude.[74]

To ensure the structural integrity and earthquake resistance of the edifice, a collaborative effort involving various expert entities was undertaken. Notably, the assessment of soil strength was conducted in consultation with IIT Madras, while earthquake-resistant design considerations were contributed by the CBRI. Champat Rai emphasized that the design of the Ram Temple in Ayodhya was aimed at ensuring maintenance-free durability for a thousand years. Rai underlined the temple's strength by highlighting its ability to withstand an earthquake of a magnitude of 6.5 on the Richter scale.[75] Vinod Kumar Mehta, the project director at L&T, confirmed the establishment of a solid foundation, reaching a depth of 15 ft, using hefty stones, thus safeguarding the temple against seismic forces without any compromise.[76]

The Trust had established an expert committee comprising distinguished engineers to provide recommendations and insights. This committee, chaired by former IIT Delhi director V.S. Raju and convened by N. Gopal Krishnan of CBRI Roorkee, comprised eminent figures such as S.R. Gandhi of NIT Surat, T.G. Sitharam of IIT Guwahati, B. Bhattacharjee of IIT Delhi, A.P. Mull of TCE, Manu Samthanam of IIT Madras and Pradipta Banerji of IIT Mumbai. The committee was granted access to comprehensive details and reports, including those from L&T and TCE, encompassing architectural and structural design, soil investigations and pile test results. L&T conducted thorough soil investigations through Cengrs Geotechnica Pvt Ltd. TCE assumed responsibility for reviewing and certifying the proposed foundation design by L&T. Essential data and documents necessary for design review were diligently provided by L&T to TCE.

The final foundation design, meticulously shaped through soil testing and analysis of superstructure loads, featured a plain cement concrete raft resting upon approximately 1,200 cement concrete piles, extending to depths of 20–40 m with a diameter of about 1 m. This design underwent rigorous examination and validation by IIT Chennai, NIT Surat and CBRI Roorkee. As mentioned earlier, the temple's design has been conceived in such a manner that it is mainly constructed using stone slabs with minimal use of cement or iron.

COUNTDOWN TO PRAN PRATISHTHA

Over a period of three exhaustive years, the remarkable journey of constructing the Ram Temple in Ayodhya has

been continuing at an impressive pace, instilling confidence
that the project will be successfully concluded within the set
timeline. There have been many steps in this journey towards
the pran pratishtha ceremony which have been summarized
below.

TABLE 1
2020: SPIRITUAL GENESIS AND MATERIAL
FOUNDATIONS—THE JOURNEY TOWARDS RAM
TEMPLE CONSTRUCTION

25 March	Lord Ram Lalla is moved to a new wooden-built mandir, 150 m away from the original site.
21 May	Excavations at the Ram Janmabhoomi Complex uncover historical treasures: 5-ft shivalinga, stone-crafted artifacts, flowers, kalash, aamalaks and doorjamb; seven pillars of black touchstone; six sturdy columns of red sandstone; broken idols of revered devi–devtas, etc.[77]
5 August	Ram Mandir bhoomi pujan is conducted. Prime Minister Modi worships nine shilas associated with the Ram Temple Movement during 1989–90.[78] This marks the commencement of construction work with a meticulous focus on soil testing, design insights and concrete quality advice from experts.[79]
2 September	Ayodhya Development Authority, in its board meeting, approves the final map of the proposed structure of Shri Ram Janmabhoomi Mandir.[80]
10 October	Relocation of meticulously carved stones from the Karsevakpuram workshop to the temple precincts starts.[81]

12 December	The Trust sets up an eight-member expert panel to supervise Ram temple foundation-laying work.[82] Discussions and meetings among stakeholders and experts take place to address foundation design, geotechnical insights and the use of engineered materials.
29 December	Meeting to discuss the open excavation process for the temple's foundation structure and the use of engineered materials is held.[83]

TABLE 2
2021: SACRED SOIL TO SOLID FOUNDATION—THE CONSTRUCTION COMMENCES

15 January	VHP in coordination with Shri Ram Janmabhoomi Teerth Kshetra Trust starts a massive 45 days fund-raising drive. The door-to-door campaign to collect contributions for the Ram Temple fund, known as the Samarpan Drive is initiated from 400 different locations.
6 February	Agreements with M/s C.B. Sompura validated for architectural design services. Agreements with Larsen & Toubro Ltd and Tata Consulting Engineers Ltd as design and building contractors and project manager consultants are also validated.[84]
17 May	The Kurma Shila Pujan is held: Nine consecrated shilas—silver and copper urns worshipped by PM Modi during the bhoomi pujan on 5 August 2020—are positioned at the foundation of the Ram Temple's garbha griha. Notably, the *kurma shila* (foundation stone carrying the symbol of a tortoise) holds special importance as the idol of Ram Lalla is to be installed on top of this very shila.[85]

31 May	The temple's foundation is constructed using the Roller Compacted Concrete (RCC) technique, with 120,000 cu. m of debris being removed.
29 August	Former President Shri Ramnath Kovind graces the Shri Ram Janmabhoomi Complex and offeres his reverence to Bhagwan Shri Ram Lalla Virajman. A sapling—a symbol of growth—is planted by him in the complex.
15 October	Base work commences, with plinth cast and roller-compacted concrete added to strengthen the foundation.
17 September	First phase of the foundation construction of the temple is completed, with the filling of the forty-eighth layer of compact concrete. This raises the temple foundation to 107 m above sea level.[86]

TABLE 3
2022: CHRONICLES OF PROGRESS—ON THE PATH OF SHRI RAM JANMABHOOMI TEMPLE CONSTRUCTION

13 January	Captivating 3D cinematic virtual 'walk-through' presentation of the proposed structure of Ram Temple is released by the Trust's YouTube channel on Lohri.[87]
24 January	Commencement of placing ~17,000 granite stones (5x2.5x3 ft, ~2.50 tonnes each) upon the raft for temple flooring.
5 April	Rajasthan's carved stone slabs reach Ayodhya for Ram Temple construction.[88] These pink stones mined at Rajasthan's Bansi Paharpur are to be used for the walls of Ram Mandir after the plinth work completion.

1 June	Uttar Pradesh CM Yogi Adityanath performs the shila pujan, thus laying the foundation of the sanctum sanctorum of the temple.
23 October	Prime Minister performs darshan and puja of Shri Ram Lalla before launching the Deepotsav Mahotsav in Ayodhya on the occasion of Diwali.[89]
October– November	The Trust lays out a comprehensive master plan for the remaining area, including the construction of various temples like those dedicated to renowned figures from the Ramayana, such as Rishi Valmiki, Acharya Vashisth, Rishi Vishwamitra, Agastya Rishi, Nishad Raj, Jatayu, Mata Sabri; along with the establishment of facilities for pilgrims, like Yagya Mandap, Anusthan Mandap, Sant Niwas, a museum, research centre and library.[90]

2023: PREPARATION FOR PRAN PRATISHTHA

As advised by experts, the choice of using sagwan wood from Ballarpur in Maharashtra's Chandrapur district for crafting the temple gates had been made in the first quarter of 2023. Accordingly, the wood consignment departed following a pujan performed by saints and devotees. The meticulously planned trial phase for door placement includes plans for 18 doors on the ground floor. (In total, the Ram Temple will have 36 doors—18 on each floor.) Two staircases, each adorned with two doors, are under construction at the front of the ground floor. The final phase will witness the expertise of gold-plating artisans, ensuring the perfect embellishment of the temple's doors.[91]

Captivating images released in the media showcased the building of doors, frames and towering 20-ft high walls, each shaping the temple's grandeur. Standing steadfast in the sanctum sanctorum are the erected pillars, bearing witness to the craftsmanship that adorns the edifice. Among the visual tapestry are the iconic Singhdwar and ornate pillars, lending their exquisite touch to the construction. As the journey unfolds, 200 meticulously carved beams are being installed within the sanctum sanctorum. These beams, crafted with artistry and devotion, find their origin in the workshops nestled within Karsevakpuram and Ramghat. The process of placing beams on the temple's plinth had been initiated earlier. After which, the endeavour to place beams above the ground floor pillars commenced.

On 12 May, a visual delight was shared with the world, as Champat Rai, with a sense of pride and accomplishment, unveiled the intricately designed roofs of the Shri Ram Janmabhoomi Temple through his Twitter (now X) handle. In a resounding testament to the progress achieved, he joyfully conveyed that the roof work was being meticulously accomplished, further adding to the grandeur of the temple. Within the Ram Temple, the walls themselves are to serve as canvases for enchanting portrayals of diverse religious motifs. This selection of themes, a collaborative effort involving spiritual leaders, artistic connoisseurs and even delegates from the prestigious Indira Gandhi National Centre for the Arts in New Delhi, will culminate in the discerning curation of the visual narratives to be depicted.

After the completion of the temple's foundation raft and plinth, the placement of Rajasthan's Bansi Paharpur stone on the three-storey temple is underway. As of July 2023, as a per a report, it was only the flooring and electrical work on the complex's ground floor housing the sanctum sanctorum that remained.[92] The management of the Trust increased the number of workers to 1,600 from 550 to ensure that the doors of the shrine can be thrown open for devotees within the stipulated time. Work, which was earlier being done in 18-hour shifts, is now being carried out round the clock.

The first floor's construction commenced in July. Its architectural essentials, the very keystones of its existence—slabs and pillars—are projected to stand in harmonious completion by the end of the year. Yet, the anticipation for entry to the first floor shall linger till the embrace of March in the year 2024, an interval attributed to some unfinished work. Champat Rai has repeatedly emphasized that construction endeavours will persist harmoniously alongside devotees' visits to the temple, reassuring that no disruptions will arise. Rain occasionally took centre stage, disrupting the outdoor orchestration of the parkota. Yet, resilience echoed within these walls, for even amidst the rain, the indoor work continued without fail.

The restoration of the ancient Kuber Tila along with the finalization of a Shiva temple and the envisioned Jatayu addition is expected to draw devotees, as previously communicated through an official statement.

In a noteworthy development on 26 August, a 600-kg, 4-ft shivalinga of Lord Narmadeshwar Mahadev arrived in Ayodhya from Omkareshwar in Madhya Pradesh. General Secretary Champat Rai, received the shivalinga with due rituals and performed a *rudrabhishek* (sacred bath) ceremony. Rai revealed that amid the Janmabhoomi complex's expansion, six temples were being established, including a Shiva complex where the Narmadeshwar Mahadev shivalinga would find its place. This shivalinga, originating from the banks of the Narmada River, had been sculpted into its shivalinga form over a three-month period. [93]

Around the time of Diwali 2023, the final touches were put on the completion of the ground floor, marking a significant milestone in the Ram Temple's construction. As mentioned earlier, according to the temple trust's comprehensive plan, the ultimate architectural layout envisions the incorporation of various temples dedicated to revered deities such as Surya, Ganesha, Shiva, Durga, Vishnu and Brahma, all within the expansive temple premises. Within the sanctum sanctorum, the idol of Ram Lalla will grace an impressive eight-foot-tall marble throne adorned with gold plating. Meticulously crafted by artisans in Rajasthan, this majestic throne is expected to arrive in Ayodhya by 15 December. Simultaneously, the completion of the ground floor is scheduled for the same date.

A dedicated workforce is tirelessly engaged in round-the-clock efforts encompassing tasks ranging from the installation of sturdy pillars and intricately designed arches to the meticulous carving of intricate reliefs and the refining of surfaces.

In a significant development in October 2023, the Ministry of Home Affairs extended its approval to the Shri Ram Janmabhoomi Teerth Kshetra Trust, [94] opening the doors for donations from around the world to contribute to the construction of the Ram Temple in Ayodhya. This not only marks a milestone in the physical creation of the temple but also signifies a global outpouring of emotional investment from individuals residing outside the country, reaffirming the deep and widespread attachment to the revered figure of Ram and the cultural legacy of Ayodhya.

On the momentous Vijaya Dashami of 2023, Prime Minister Narendra Modi shared in a speech that it was the country's great fortune that the citizens were witnessing the grandeur of the construction of Lord Ram's temple.[95] He said that as we approached the upcoming Ram Navami in Ayodhya, the resounding aura of Lord Ram's divine abode would fill the air, spreading joy across the entire world, and that the imminent arrival of Lord Shri Ram in Ayodhya's Ram Temple promised a sacred moment, destined to bring delight to the global community. Reflecting on the symbolic burning of Ravana, the PM articulated that this act should transcend a mere effigy, representing the eradication of distortions disrupting societal harmony, and that it must symbolize the elimination of forces fostering division in the name of caste and region and the extinguishing of ideologies prioritizing personal gain over national progress. Vijayadashami, he emphasized, was not solely a celebration of Ram's triumph over Ravana but a festival that champions national unity against all adversities. Prime Minister Modi's Dussehra address, especially in the context of the Ram Temple, struck a chord as it embodied the essence of unity and collective advancement.

DIVINE HOMECOMING: PRAN PRATISHTHA SPECTACLE IN THE OFFING

In a tale woven with historical threads and sacred aspirations, the Shri Ram Janambhoomi Trust penned an illustrious chapter by extending an earnest invitation to PM Narendra Modi.[96] The invitation, adorned with the significance of consecrating Lord Ram's idol in the sanctum sanctorum of the Ram Mandir in Ayodhya on 22 January, was met with a jubilant acceptance from the PM. The digital realm buzzed with the news as PM Narendra Modi expressed a profound sense of gratitude to partake in this epochal moment.[97] As the Trust and PM Modi conversed in a meeting filled with emotions, the confirmation of the pran pratishtha ceremony on 22 January added another golden leaf to the book of Ayodhya's spiritual journey. The Trust leadership also personally extended their invitation to CM Yogi Adityanath, which he graciously accepted.

In a historic and emotionally charged appeal on 3 November broadcasted across social media platforms, the Trust extended a heartfelt invitation to devotees worldwide for the momentous ceremony.[98] The ceremony, as announced, has been scheduled on the auspicious day of Poush Shukla Dwadashi, Vikram Samvat 2080, falling on Monday, 22 January 2024, to be unfolded between 11.00 a.m. and 1.00 p.m. Whether within the sacred environs of a nearby temple or in the intimate spaces of personal abodes, devotees were invited to join in the spiritual fervour. The ceremony has been planned to be broadcasted live on Doordarshan, ensuring that devotees across the globe could witness and participate in this monumental event. The call to devotion spanned continents, creating a shared feeling that united hearts in a collective journey toward the historic pran pratishtha.

The seventh edition of the 'Deepotsav' or Diwali festival, organized with grandeur and excitement by the UP government in Ayodhya, was a spectacle to behold. The under-construction Ram Temple, adorned with marigold flowers, various blooms and radiant diyas, emanated an exuberant aura, offering a glimpse of the grandeur it will assume on the consecration day when Shri Ram returns from his 500-year Kaliyuga vanvaas.[99] The Shri Ram Janmabhoomi Path, embellished with flowers and diyas, added to the festive ambience. The path, illuminated by 22.23 lakh earthen lamps, witnessed Ayodhya's 'Deepotsav' creating a new Guinness World Record, further enhancing the enchantment of the festivities.[100] On the luminous occasion of Diwali, CM Yogi Adityanath envisioned Ayodhya transforming into the world's most enchanting city. With profound symbolism, he performed the coronation of Lord Shri Ram, underscoring the pivotal role of the Ram Temple in crafting the ideals of Ram-Rajya in India. Chief Minister Yogi, with a resolute spirit, called upon the people of Ayodhya to embark upon early preparations for the momentous event on 22 January, invoking the cherished ethos of 'Atithi Devo Bhava'.[101]

Shri Alok Kumar, the working president of VHP, addressed a press conference on 13 November in New Delhi, to announce global programmes related to Shri Ram Janmabhoomi, where he stated:

> The first program is on January 22... In this, we have asked people from around the world to assume that your neighbouring temple is Ayodhya and go and watch the ceremony there collectively... In nearly 5 lakh temples, approximately 7 crore or more Hindus will watch the consecration of Lord Ram (idol). After that, we will take people from every state who took part in this fight (for the construction of the temple) and who have passed away but whose families are there, to seek darshan and

fulfil our duty towards them. Nearly 1 lakh people will be able to seek darshan from this scheme.[102]

Overall, these global programmes mark a momentous step in uniting the worldwide Sanatan community and commemorating the cultural significance of Shri Ram Janmabhoomi. It can be seen that, through these initiatives, VHP is forging a symbolic bond that transcends geographical boundaries. In the preceding months as well, in anticipation of the grand consecration of Ram Lalla at Ram Janmabhoomi in January 2024, the VHP orchestrated more than 2,500 *'shaurya yatras'* (valour procession) across the country between 30 September and 15 October, spanning all districts in UP.[103] These yatras aimed to enlighten people about the temple movement's history and update them on the progress of the Ram Temple construction.

In an unprecedented gesture, PM Narendra Modi is poised to defy protocol, embarking on a momentous walk of over 500 m. This extraordinary stroll will witness him personally carrying the revered idol of Ram Lalla from the existing makeshift temple to the grandeur of the newly erected Ram Mandir during the much-anticipated pran pratishtha ceremony. A report revealed that PM Modi might graciously accept the esteemed responsibility of carrying the current movable idol of Ram Lalla, consecrating it within the sacred confines of the newly constructed temple.[104] Joining this sacred procession, UP CM Yogi Adityanath and RSS chief, Mohan Bhagwat are expected to add their august presence to the auspicious occasion.[105]

As the temple trust meticulously orchestrates this historic affair, an extensive guest list will bring together a diverse spectrum of attendees. Meanwhile, Ayodhya is abuzz with preparations for various momentous ceremonies, such as the recently organized Akshat Puja on 5 November 2023. During this Akshat Puja, turmeric-coloured *akshat* (rice) was ceremoniously presented to Ram Lalla, marking the inaugural ritual in the prelude to the grand pran pratishtha ceremony. This sanctified Akshat is planned to be taken to every village temple in India.

THE ULTIMATE VISION REALIZED

The remaining construction journey for the temple is to unfold in three pivotal phases. The initial phase, triumphantly achieved by December 2023, encompasses the establishment of the six temples situated around the central theme of Lord Ram, as well as the completion of the ground floor, excluding the intricate iconography. Subsequently, the second phase encompasses the meticulous construction of the first and second floors, a feat set to grace completion by December 2024. The grand culmination of this intricate and reverent project is anticipated to finish by 2025, by which time the entire complex will have been, with great care, brought to its full fruition.

Within the embrace of the temple's architecture lies a profound reflection of broader societal values. In a conversation with *Hindustan Times*, Nripendra Mishra, chairman of the construction committee, highlighted two facets of the Ram Temple being constructed that have been taken from PM Narendra Modi's insights. Prime Minister Modi's words resonate with depth as he underlines that Ram's elevation to 'Maryada Purshottam' came after his return from exile. This essence, encapsulating Lord Ram's journey, finds its expression through the meticulously crafted murals adorning the temple's outer boundary—a dynamic depiction of those who lived up to the highest ideals of his legacy. A second facet, beautifully orchestrated, involves six temples outside the main complex. These temples enshrine figures that stand as beacons of inclusivity and harmony. The temple emerges as a profound testament of *'samarasta'*—social harmony—reflecting India's vision of a united, shared heritage. Nripendra Mishra has earnestly conveyed that the temple invites not just those who identify as Hindu, but all seekers, fostering a space where personal faith converges into a common understanding of culture.[106]

Champat Rai beautifully illuminates the profound vision of PM Narendra Modi encapsulated within the Ayodhya Ram Temple project. Prime Minister Modi, through his sagacious insight, proposed a consecrated space within the temple's precincts for revered figures like Shabari, Nishadraj, Jatayu and Ahilya, since their intrinsic significance in Lord Shri Ram's saga as integral companions of his journey, is deeply acknowledged by all. With Lord Ram's lineage tracing back to the Sooryavansh dynasty—the sun's descendant—a novel notion emerged: Could the sun's rays bless Ram Lalla at high noon? This idea of PM Modi was presented to Council of Scientific and Industrial Research (CSIR), yielding fruitful success through its adoption.

As the temple's construction surges forth, it magnificently embodies the values of unity, devotion and a far-reaching vision. With over 1,600 dedicated artisans tirelessly crafting the temple's pillars, arches and intricate details, the temple becomes more than just a structure—it becomes a living embodiment of faith. As the temple's completion draws nearer, it stands as a harmonizing force, a place where diverse beliefs converge and the echoes of unity resound, transcending the divides of history and uniting people in shared devotion and a vision for a harmonious future.

The Ayodhya Ram Temple will not only stand as a beacon of faith but also as a cultural testament to Lord Ram's multi-faceted persona. Beyond the sacred sanctum sanctorum that houses Lord Ram's divine idol, the temple complex will host a captivating exhibition, an eloquent reflection of both the 'philosophy' and the 'humanity' of Lord Ram. This specially curated showcase, aptly themed 'Ram: The Man and the Idea', will be a gathering of artistic masterpieces contributed by no less than 75 distinguished artists from across the nation. In this artistic ensemble, the vibrant canvases and sculptures will paint a vivid portrait of Lord Ram's multifaceted personality and the ideals he embodies. The exhibition promises to be an enriching experience, a journey into the heart of Lord Ram's philosophy, his humane attributes and his timeless resonance in the tapestry of human ideals.

5

ECHOES OF TRETA IN AYODHYA: ANCIENT LEGACY, MODERN TRANSFORMATION

Ayodhya, nestled at the geographical coordinates 24° 94' N latitude and 82° 12' E longitude[1], is poised for a remarkable transformation that promises to etch its name on the global tourist map. This once-sleepy city is now riding the crest of a real estate boom, driven by the monumental Ram Janmabhoomi Mandir project. Like a phoenix rising from the ashes, a new chapter of development has ushered in Ayodhya.

Furthermore, the 2022 UP tourism policy envisages that all places associated with Lord Ram will be developed as a Ramayana tourist circuit. The Ramayana circuit will include Ayodhya, Chitrakoot, Bithoor and other religious places, as these sites are seen as symbols of Lord Ram and Mother Sita. Under UP's visionary tourism policy, a staggering 89 companies have expressed their interest in Ayodhya's blossoming tourism sector, with 26 projects receiving the coveted green signal.[2] The calendar marks January 2024 as the month when the inaugural ceremony of the grand Ram Temple's first phase will transpire, a historic moment that is already sending ripples through the city.

Uttar Pradesh CM Yogi Adityanath, painting a vivid picture of Ayodhya's ascendancy, proudly declared it as one of the world's most coveted destinations for tourists, whether they hail from India's heartland or the far reaches of the globe. As the Ram Temple nears completion, Ayodhya's charm has lured the behemoths of the hospitality industry from India and beyond. Each day sees a surge in pilgrim footfall, mirrored by a simultaneous surge in new hotel constructions. Taj's parent company, Indian Hotels Company Ltd (IHCL) has announced signing of a 100-room upscale Vivanta and 120-room 'lean luxe' Ginger in the holy town which will open by 2027.[3] With expectations of an infrastructure boom, Ayodhya's land prices have soared to unprecedented heights, setting off a frenzy of land deals and ushering in a flurry of hotel constructions and infrastructure development, all at an astonishing pace.[4]

In the wake of the Supreme Court's historic verdict in 2019, property rates in Ayodhya's heart surged into the range of ₹2,000–3,000 per sq. ft, while even in its hinterlands, they catapulted to an impressive ₹1,000–1,500 per sq. ft within a year. This whirlwind of activity is fuelled by the anticipation of a tourism boom once the magnificent Ram Temple graces the cityscape, drawing both government and private investors to hastily craft infrastructure and hospitality offerings. Ayodhya seems ready to emerge as what may be termed a spiritual tourist destination.[5]

GOVERNMENT ENDEAVOURS: PAVING THE WAY FOR AYODHYA'S RENAISSANCE

The ancient city steeped in history, is undergoing a breathtaking transformation that comes with an estimated price tag of a staggering ₹30,000 crore, all part of the grand 'Ayodhya Vision 2047'. This ambitious endeavour, orchestrated jointly by the state and central governments, encompasses a mosaic of nearly 260 projects, spanning the realms of tourism, aviation, infrastructure, housing, healthcare, energy, culture, urban development, transport, and more.[6] It's an awe-inspiring tapestry of progress, a canvas upon which Ayodhya redefines itself for the future.[7] This colossal figure doesn't account for the monumental task of constructing the divine abode of Lord Ram, the Ram Temple, as it is being sculpted through the devotees' donations under the guardianship of the Shri Ram Janmabhoomi Teerth Kshetra Trust.

The anticipation of a deluge of pilgrims and tourists thronging to Ayodhya post the Ram Temple's completion in January 2024 has catalyzed a wave of transformation. In March 2023, the UP cabinet, presided over by CM Yogi Adityanath, approved infrastructural and hospitality projects worth ₹465 crore. Among these projects is the expansion and embellishment of the Dharma Path, a 2-km road stretching from NH-27 to Naya Ghat, designed to be an inviting passage for pilgrims and travellers alike. The plan also includes the creation of amenities and serene resting spots for tourists, transformations of approximately 9 km of Pancha Kosi Parikrama Marg, and 24 km of 14 Kosi Parikrama Marg into a four-lane route. But this is merely the overture to Ayodhya's grand symphony. With its sight set on becoming the model temple town of the future, CM Yogi Adityanath, on 15 July 2023, unfurled the banner of progress and inaugurated another set of 44 projects valued at ₹212.5 crore, a testament to Ayodhya's journey from the past into a radiant tomorrow. To further underline this commitment, he laid the foundation for 38 transformative projects, valued at an astounding ₹1,763.2 crore, destined to breathe life into Ayodhya's dreams.[8] In this process of transformation, Ayodhya emerges not just as a city but as a crucible of heritage and progress, a beacon of devotion and innovation, and a testament to what human endeavour can achieve when fuelled by faith and determination.

MARYADA PURUSHOTTAM SHRI RAM INTERNATIONAL AIRPORT

Ayodhya's skies are set to become a gateway to this spiritual world. The Maryada Purushottam Shri Ram International Airport, a vision brought to life, is poised to welcome dignitaries and devotees alike. This 821-acre marvel near the Lucknow–Gorakhpur highway, is set to make its debut on the global stage before the Ram Temple unveils its sanctum in January 2024. The Airports Authority of India (AAI), in collaboration with the UP civil aviation department, is orchestrating this aviation progress. With 793 acres already secured and construction of the first phase well underway, this airport signifies a monumental shift. Initially, a 2,200-meter runway will allow only small aircraft catering to 60 passengers to land in Ayodhya, the final phase, which is slated for completion by 2025, will welcome giants like the Boeing aircraft. As the terminal building takes shape, it has been designed to echo the grandeur of the Ram Temple, a homage to the city's spiritual significance. AAI officials proudly proclaim that the airport's entrance and main building will serve as a living testament to Ayodhya's cultural legacy.

In its first phase, this airport will be dedicated to domestic operations, with a grand domestic terminal spanning 6,000 sq. m and equipped to handle 300 peak-hour passengers, complete with three aerobridges. This project was ushered into reality when the UP civil aviation department leased 317.855 acres of land to the AAI in April 2022. Today, with the runway nearly complete, the airport's elevation resembles the spiritual beacon it stands beside, and its ambitions soar just as high.

THE REVAMPED RAILWAY STATION

The heart of Ayodhya's rail connectivity, the Ayodhya Dham Railway Station, is undergoing a remarkable transformation. This ambitious project includes the development of three new platforms set to grace the station by December this year, followed by landscaping of the area and the creation of another railway track in the second phase. The project comes with a price tag of ₹200 crore, a testament to the government's commitment to Ayodhya's progress.

The existing Ayodhya railway station itself is undergoing a revamp that's bound to turn heads. At a cost of ₹443 crore, this project embodies Ayodhya's essence, drawing inspiration from the sacred Shri Ram Janmabhoomi Temple. Its design showcases domes, soaring *shikhars* (spires), and towering pillars—a reverent nod to the city's spiritual significance.

The transformation unfolds in two phases. The first phase encompasses a double-storied building, a resplendent metal shed, expansive circulating areas, two foot overbridges, a dormitory, an infirmary, escalators, elevators, a food court, air-conditioned retiring rooms, LED billboards and various other amenities. As the first phase nears completion by the end of this year or early next year, the railway station will cater to a staggering 25,000 passengers daily. This surge in capacity will prove invaluable during auspicious occasions like Dussehra, Ram Navami, Diwali, and more. The second phase will focus on crafting spacious waiting and parking areas for pilgrims in the southern part of the railway station, further elevating the station's utility and enhancing the experience for travellers and devotees.

THE BUS TERMINAL

Back in June 2021, the UP cabinet gave its resounding approval for a remarkable project—the construction of a bus station in Ayodhya complying with international standards, a masterpiece expected to cost ₹400 crore.[9] As the city gears up for the completion of the monumental Ram Temple, special emphasis is placed on enhancing transportation facilities. Approximately nine acres of land, graciously offered by the Department of Culture, will be seamlessly transferred to the Department of Transport, serving as the canvas for this visionary bus station. Plans are afoot to potentially develop it through a Public–Private Partnership (PPP) model, nestled near the 'Sanskriti Manch', a cultural gem currently taking shape. The essence of this grand project lies in its role in facilitating pilgrims and tourists. It will not only enhance connectivity within the region but also strengthen the links to other prominent parts of Uttar Pradesh, including Prayagraj, Gorakhpur, Varanasi, Ballia, Lucknow, Azamgarh, Kanpur, and others. At the heart of this transformation lies the 84 Kosi Parikrama Marg, a monumental 236-km-long highway connecting the Awadh districts of Ayodhya, Barabanki, Gonda, Basti and Ambedkarnagar. With an investment of ₹3,164 crore, this highway will facilitate the sacred circumambulations or parikramas undertaken by devout pilgrims. Alongside the highway, a 5.5-meter-wide walkway will be constructed, providing a safe and convenient route for those partaking in the parikrama.

Another vital artery in Ayodhya's new road network is the Pratapgarh–Sultanpur–Ayodhya state highway, set for expansion into a four-lane road. This development is part of a broader initiative to bolster Ayodhya's transportation infrastructure. The proposed four-lane Ayodhya–Varanasi highway, a 65-km-long ring road costing ₹2,588 crores,[10] and the creation of the 262-km-long Ram Van Gaman Marg from Ayodhya to Chitrakoot, allotted with ₹2,020 crore,[11] are integral components of this ambitious effort.

In a bid to reduce traffic congestion on the Lucknow–Gorakhpur highway, the National Highways Authority of India (NHAI) is crafting a 65-km-long outer ring road. This four-lane marvel will pass through Ayodhya, Gonda and Basti, offering a streamlined route for travellers. This comprehensive endeavour also incorporates three distinct pathways:

- Janmabhoomi Path: A 0.566 km four-lane road, stretching from Sugriva Fort to Shri Ram Janmabhoomi Mandir Marg

- Bhakti Path: A 0.742 km four-lane road from Shringar Haat to Shri Ram Janmabhoomi Mandir Marg
- Ram Path: A road spanning 12.94 km from Sahadatganj to Naya Ghat Marg. It will be named Ram Path to facilitate access to the Lord Shri Ram Janmabhoomi Temple.

The scale of Ayodhya's ongoing transformation becomes evident when one traverses its streets. As one approaches the Naya Ghat crossing (now the Lata Mangeshkar crossing) the city is abuzz with activity. Nearly 900 labourers are toiling around the clock to widen three key roads. The 13-km stretch from Naya Ghat to Sahadatganj is part of this expansive project, encompassing the arterial road connecting Ayodhya Dham with Ayodhya. Approximately 800 shops and residences have made way for the 13-km-long Ram Path, surrounding the temple.

The UP government has set an ambitious deadline of December 2023 for completing all pathways in Ayodhya. It has also given a green light to the expansion of the Panch Kosi, which traverses Ayodhya city, and the 14 Kosi Parikrama Marg encircling its outskirts. While these projects necessitate the demolition of around 2,600 houses and commercial establishments, they reflect the comprehensive approach taken to revitalize Ayodhya's infrastructure. As of 2023, the entire route of the Panch Kosi, 14 Kosi and 84 Kosi parikramas are under development, accompanied by renovations of religious sites along their paths.[12]

Ayodhya's journey into modernity, marked by a harmonious blend of tradition and progress, stands as a testament to the UP government's unwavering commitment to preserving its rich heritage while welcoming an ever-increasing number of spiritual seekers. With an investment exceeding ₹30,000 crore, Ayodhya is not merely evolving; it is embracing the future while cherishing its timeless traditions.

Thus, the air, rail and road connectivity to Ayodhya is all set for a remarkable transition and is in the process of development, as befits a major tourist and spiritual destination. Enhancing physical connectivity is just one facet of the boost in infrastructure in Ayodhya. There is much more to this aspect which is described in detail further in this chapter.

NAVYA AYODHYA TOWNSHIP

In response to the environmental concerns regarding the infrastructural development of Ayodhya, Dr Jaswant Singh, director of the Institute of Earth and Environmental Sciences at Dr Rammanohar Lohia Avadh University in Ayodhya, states that there is an extensive tree-plantion initiative underway at designated sites to create a more natural atmosphere. Additionally, efforts are in progress to rejuvenate water bodies associated with the Ramayana. Within the grand temple complex, trees such as deodar, mango, red sandalwood, banyan, ashok, and others mentioned in the epic will be cultivated.[13] With regard to the same, in the heartland of Ayodhya, a vibrant canvas of aspirations unfolds as the UP Housing and Development Board embarks on an extraordinary venture—Navya Ayodhya, or 'new' Ayodhya, a sprawling 1,200-acre township.[14] This visionary project paints a picture of eco-friendly living, seamlessly blending tradition and modernity. At its core lies the creation of opulent state guest houses, welcoming visitors with open arms. Land auctions will soon follow, offering prime real estate for the construction of luxury hotels, while residential plots will find their place in the sun after the meticulous development of roads, sewage systems and drainage networks.

The essence of the ambitious venture of Navya Ayodhya transcends mere bricks and mortar. It harbours a 'Nirvana Abode', a haven for those on the precipice of eternity, seeking moksha or salvation. The initiative includes offering studio apartments along the banks of the sacred Sarayu River for those seeking to embrace the end of their life in Ayodhya. These studio apartments are to be priced between ₹20–25 lakh each. For those who may face financial constraints, there's an option to make a partial payment, with an agreement that the unit reverts to the authority after the allottee's passing.[15] The introduction of the 'moksha destination'[16] plan not only showcases the innovative urban planning approach within Navya Ayodhya but also reflects a unique intertwining of spiritual and residential aspects. By providing a space for individuals to contemplate their final journey in Ayodhya, the city is fostering a deeper connection between life, spirituality and the environment. This initiative not only addresses the practical aspects of housing but also touches upon the profound cultural and spiritual essence of Ayodhya, contributing to its ongoing spiritual transformation.

Apart from the spiritual aspect, the township boldly marries the ancient with the modern. A 'National Avenue' adorned with State Bhawans or state guest houses and an 'International Avenue' hosting Country Bhawans or international guest houses are poised to grace the township's landscape, reminiscent of Delhi's Chanakyapuri. Spanning 1,500 acres, the upcoming township is set to become a cultural haven with guest houses representing nearly two dozen states. Among its diverse offerings are guest houses tailored for five countries, including Korea, as well as monasteries and over 100 plots designated for various sects, communities and volunteer organizations. This meticulously planned township not only caters to the vibrant tapestry of Indian traditions but also extends a warm invitation to NRIs and foreigners seeking an immersive experience in the rich tapestry of Indian heritage. With its array of accommodations and facilities, the township aims to be a melting pot where diverse cultures converge, fostering a unique and inclusive atmosphere. Anticipating a steady influx of tourists from different states and countries, these Bhavans offer a welcoming haven for these visitors. The township promises a symphony of cultural experiences. A spellbinding 7D Ramlila, a mesmerizing light and sound odyssey recounting the epic Ramayana and a soul-stirring musical fountain, serenading the verses of the Hanuman Chalisa, are expected to create a tapestry of enchantment.[17] With a rich tapestry of offerings, Navya Ayodhya aspires to become a 'spiritual destination', drawing travellers from every corner of the world, weaving its unique narrative into the global traveller's tale. It's a promise, an ode to tradition and a journey into the future, all in one—an odyssey that paints the skies and the landscape of Ayodhya in vibrant hues.

SHRI RAM STATUE

The UP government, under the guidance of CM Yogi Adityanath, is embarking on a monumental project—an awe-inspiring statue that will pierce the skies and touch the heavens. Beyond its sheer height, it's destined to surpass all expectations. Alongside the statue, a mesmerizing complex will take shape—a digital museum, a sanctum in the theme of Lord Ram's life, an interpretation centre that unravels the mystique of his life and teachings, a library echoing with the wisdom of the ages, a food plaza tantalizing the senses with delectable offerings and ample parking space to welcome the faithful and the curious alike. This colossal attempt has garnered international acclaim, and to ensure its successful realization, the UP government has joined hands with the government of Gujarat.[18] A Memorandum of Understanding (MoU) is on the horizon, promising technical expertise and guidance from Gujarat. The vision for the Ram statue will draw inspiration from the successful Gujarat model, notably exemplified by the construction of the colossal Sardar Patel statue. This strategic partnership is poised to elevate the execution of the project, blending innovation and proven methodologies to bring the envisioned Ram statue to life with finesse and precision. As the sun sets and the stars illuminate the night sky over Ayodhya, this monumental statue will stand as a sentinel, a guardian of the city's spiritual heritage, a testament to the enduring legacy of Lord Ram and a source of inspiration for generations to come.

JATAYU CRUISE SERVICE

As the sacred city of Ayodhya prepares to unveil the magnificent Ram Mandir to the world, it is also charting new waters, quite literally. Before the temple's grand opening in January, Ayodhya is embarking on a journey of a different kind. The 'Jatayu' luxury cruise service which has started from 8 September 2023, is a testament to Ayodhya's commitment to offering visitors an unforgettable experience. As it gracefully glides on the serene waters of the Sarayu, this cruise becomes a floating window to the city's history and spirituality.[19] Starting from the historic Guptar Ghat, passengers embark on a mesmerizing two-hour journey, akin to the celebrated cruises in Varanasi. Along the way, the past and present of Ayodhya merge in a seamless blend of scenic beauty and historical significance. Raj Ghat, Laxman Ghat, Ram Ghat and Janki Ghat, all make their appearances, each reverberating with the legends of Lord Ram and the tales of the Ramayana. The cruise is not just about the sights it offers, it's an immersive experience. Onboard, passengers are treated to a culinary voyage, savouring the flavours of the region. Folk songs and traditional dances add a vibrant layer of entertainment, bringing Ayodhya's rich cultural heritage to life. With a maximum capacity of 100 passengers, the Jatayu cruise is set to make Ayodhya's riverfront a thriving hub of activity. It promises to be more than a mode of transport; it's a portal to the heart and soul of Ayodhya. As it meanders through the city's waters, it carries with it the hopes and dreams of a city that's ready to welcome the world.

RAMALAND

In the heart of Ayodhya, a magical realm is taking shape, poised to transport visitors into the captivating world of Lord Ram and the epic Ramayana. This enchanting place named 'Ramaland' is the UP government's visionary project to transform Ayodhya into a global tourism hotspot. Drawing inspiration from the enchanting Disneyland in California, Ramaland promises to be an educational and entertaining wonderland for people of all ages.[20] This innovative theme park, officially known as 'Ayodhya Imaginative and Prescient 2047', is expected to be an extraordinary destination, featuring modern entertainment attractions, thrilling rides and a dedicated section for religious tourism. While the amusement rides promise excitement, an 'infotainment' section will be the heart of Ramaland. Here, tourists will immerse themselves in the timeless stories of Lord Ram, gaining valuable insights into the moral values he embodied. This unique blend of entertainment and education is set to become a pivotal landmark in Ayodhya, inviting the world to discover the essence of Ramayana and the virtues of Lord Ram.[21]

TEMPLE MUSEUM

The UP government is working on a plan to establish a museum in Ayodhya that will serve as a showcase for the rich history of renowned temples throughout India. This initiative aims to promote awareness and understanding of the Hindu religion, particularly among the younger generation.[22] The temple museum will feature various galleries, each dedicated to different aspects of Hindu temples, including their architectural design and construction. These galleries will use pictures and murals to highlight the distinctive features and vibrant architecture of famous temples from across the country. Additionally, the museum will offer a light and sound show, complete with expertly crafted narrations to enhance the visitor experience. The UP Tourism Department has initiated the development of a comprehensive action plan for this museum project.

RAM CHALIT MANAS

The Ayodhya administration is embarking on a series of development projects in tandem with the construction of the temple at Lord Ram's birthplace. These initiatives are designed to accommodate the expected influx of pilgrims, starting in January 2024. One significant project entails the development of over 75 acres of land near the Sarayu River, adjacent to Guptar Ghat in Ayodhya.[23] This area is designated as the 'Shri Ram Chalit Manas' and will serve as an experiential centre equipped with world-class amenities, aimed at creating a memorable pilgrimage experience.[24]

RAM PATH: THE SHRI RAM HERITAGE WALK

The ancient city of Ayodhya, steeped in the spiritual legacy of Lord Ram, is poised to embrace the future with the transformation of its iconic Ram Path into a captivating heritage walk. Over its 13-km stretch connecting Saadatganj to Nayahat in Ayodhya, this historic pathway will soon be adorned with a stunning tapestry of 100 murals dedicated to Lord Ram, a living tribute to his timeless saga. Collaboratively curated by the Ayodhya Development Authority (ADA) and Ayodhya Sanrakshan Samiti, these intricate wall paintings and murals will breathe new life into the very stones that have witnessed the epic journey of Lord Ram. The Ayodhya administration, committed to ensuring an engaging experience for tourists, will enlist the expertise of an agency to infuse enchantment into this cultural odyssey. Ram Path's metamorphosis extends beyond artistry. It would be equipped with amenities for visitors. It will be endowed with ornate decorative lights, luminous streetlights, verdant plantations, welcoming footpaths and inviting benches. As it gracefully meanders through the city, it will not only bear witness to the profound spiritual fervour but also offer respite to those who seek solace in its tranquil ambience. Moreover, the journey to Ayodhya's spiritual heart will soon be further facilitated by the expansion of a 16.7-km road leading to the majestic 251-m-high statue of Lord Ram. This ambitious road-widening project, endorsed by the UP cabinet, promises to encapsulate the rich tapestry of Ayodhya's cultural and spiritual heritage. Along this route, pilgrims and tourists will be greeted not only by the awe-inspiring statue but also the solemn Dashrath Samadhi Sthal and a proposed theme park. Ensuring convenience, this four-lane road will serve as a bypass, allowing for smoother transit.

Intriguingly, the journey along the enhanced Ram Path will unveil the city's rejuvenated façades, aligning with façade control guidelines proposed by the local development authority. The transformation is a meticulous endeavour driven by a desire to present Ayodhya in its full splendour before the grand inauguration of the Ram Temple in January 2024. With tourists and pilgrims set to converge upon this hallowed city, the state government has issued a directive to the Public Works Department (PWD) and the ADA, charging them with the responsibility of completing all development works by 31 December 2023. Thus, Ayodhya's Ram Path, destined to bear the weight of history and the promise of a glorious future, stands as a testament to the city's readiness to embrace the world with open arms. From January onwards, it will be the scenic gateway to the temple town, beckoning travellers from the Lucknow–Gorakhpur national highway into the heart of Ayodhya's sacred embrace.

The district administration had approved expansion of three prominent roads leading to the Ram Temple in Ayodhya. Of the three roads, the longest stretch is the 13-km 'Ram Path' starting from Sahadatganj to Naya Ghat. The second longest stretch is the two-km 'Ram Janmabhoomi Path', which starts from Sugreev Quila to Ram Mandir. The shortest stretch of 0.75 km is Bhakti Path from Shringar Hat to Ram Janmabhoomi. The Ram Path is one of the three roads leading to the Ram Mandir. It is proposed to be the most beautiful stretch.

THE LOTUS FOUNTAIN

In the heart of Ayodhya, near the Guptar Ghat, a symphony of water and artistry is poised to bloom—an extraordinary lotus-shaped fountain, a testament to divine beauty and human ingenuity. The announcement of a multimedia show fountain, valued at ₹100 crore, near the upcoming Shri Ram Temple premises, propels the soon-to-be-inaugurated Ram Mandir and its surrounding premises into the global spotlight.[25] Crafted with precision, the fountain, resembling a resplendent lotus, will gracefully send waters soaring to a majestic height of 50 m. This grand spectacle recognizes the special significance of water elements within the overall concept of Shri Ram Mandir, with its seven entrances symbolizing the seven main rivers of the country. Though its completion may trail the inauguration of the Ram Mandir,

its allure promises to resonate globally. As the proposal
materializes, Ayodhya anticipates the emergence of an
enchanting masterpiece, inviting the world to witness the
unfolding saga of divine grandeur.[26]

ROOF-TOP CAFES

In the heart of Ayodhya's spiritual rebirth, a captivating
transformation unfolds, where tradition meets modernity in a
harmonious embrace. As the magnificent Ram Janmabhoomi
Mandir graces the city's skyline, a visionary concept takes
shape to elevate the pilgrim's experience to new heights—quite
literally. Cafeterias, adorned on the terraces of the houses that
encircle this resplendent temple, are poised to become not
just eateries but enchanting portals to behold the grandeur
of this sacred complex. [27] In the quest to transform Ayodhya
into a modern marvel while preserving its storied heritage,
the precincts surrounding the temple will be adorned with
artifacts that breathe life into its historical significance. And
yet, a touch of contemporary charm awaits the pilgrims and
visitors. Roof-top cafes, nestled in the houses along the Ram
Janmabhoomi Path and Bhakti Path, beckon those who seek
not just a meal but an experience, a connection with the
divine and an unparalleled view.

25 RAM STAMBHS: REFLECTION OF AYODHYA'S LEGACY

In the heart of Ayodhya, where history and spirituality
converge, a remarkable transformation is underway. The
ADA has embarked on a visionary journey to erect 25

magnificent Ram Stambhs, or pillars, along a 13-km stretch from Sahadatganj to Naya Ghat and an additional 4-km-long Dharam Path leading to the revered Ram Temple.[28] These pillars, more than mere landmarks, are poised to become the guiding beacons for countless devotees on their pilgrimage to the sacred Ram Janmabhoomi. What sets these pillars apart is not just their functional significance but the intricate stories they will tell. Each of these 6-ft-high marvels of a diameter of 5 ft will be crafted with meticulous detail, reminiscent of the ornate carvings adorning the walls of temples scattered across India. Yet, these pillars are more than just artistic endeavours; they are a reflection of Ayodhya's resplendent cultural heritage and its storied history.[29]

As the sun dips below the horizon, a breathtaking sight awaits. Atop each of these pillars, a delicate 10 mm glass light will be affixed, casting a gentle glow that dances in the night, illuminating not just the path but also the city's vibrant legacy. For these pillars are not mere structures; they are storytellers, whispering tales of devotion, tradition and the enduring spirit of Ayodhya. Every carving etched upon these pillars, every glimmer of light, every inch of their form will echo the soul of Ayodhya, and with every passing traveller, they will share the narrative of this timeless city.[30] This ambitious project, entailing an expenditure of approximately ₹2.5 crore, is not just about erecting structures; it's about breathing life into the very essence of Ayodhya, making every step of the pilgrimage a journey through history, culture and spirituality. As the Ram Temple nears completion, these pillars are poised to stand as guardians, not just of the faithful, but of Ayodhya's legacy.

AYODHYA HAAT

Ayodhya Haat, perched on the banks of the sacred Sarayu River, harmoniously blends tradition and modernity in the heart of Ayodhya.[31] Championed by the ADA, this initiative not only enriches the town's spiritual heritage but also propels it into a bustling tourist destination. Set against the picturesque backdrop of Chaudhary Charan Singh Ghat, the Haat is poised to invigorate the local economy while providing a platform for local artisans to showcase their craftsmanship. From specially designed stalls featuring intricate handicrafts to a captivating floating restaurant and serene boat services, it promises a vibrant convergence of culture and commerce. For those seeking an extended stay, Ram Kutir cottages offer riverside serenity, complemented by a convenient jetty. Cultural enthusiasts will relish captivating performances, laser shows and musical fountains. The centrepiece is an exquisite floating restaurant offering panoramic views of the Sarayu River and the grandeur of the Ram Temple, where diverse cuisines await. Boat rides along the serene Sarayu River and a spectrum of cultural programmes, from dance and music to drama and puppet shows, complete the experience.[32] With a commitment to cleanliness and sustainability, Ayodhya Haat embodies the Yogi Adityanath government's vision to elevate Ayodhya into a prominent religious and tourist destination, seamlessly bridging the past with the future.

AYODHYA ARTS PROJECT

Ayodhya is preparing for a remarkable transformation with a unique underwater art installation depicting Lord Ram's

Jal Samadhi in the Sarayu River.[33] This project, part of a broader beautification initiative, is set to bring the city's history to life through various artworks, sculptures and installations. Meenakshi Payal, project director of Mojarto, is collaborating with French artist Chifumi Krohom to create this captivating portrayal of Lord Ram submerged in the Sarayu River. The project also involves restoring the heritage structure of Ram Ki Paidi and engaging the local community, including artists and students, to participate in this historic endeavour. This beautification effort, in association with Namami Gange and in collaboration with the ADA, seeks to preserve Ayodhya's heritage and make it more appealing to tourists from around the world. The city anticipates hosting artists from various countries as it prepares for a grand Deepotsav celebration with 7.5 lakh earthen lamps being lit.

THE GLOBAL DESIGN COMPETITION

In March 2023, ADA announced the Global Design Competition aimed at transforming the city's major roads through artistic murals and sculptures.[34] This competition sought to enhance tourism and showcase Ayodhya's rich cultural heritage by inviting artists and innovators from around the world to participate.

At that time, Ayodhya was on the cusp of becoming a global religious destination, thanks in part to the imminent completion of the Shri Ram Janmabhoomi Temple. This transformative project was expected to reshape Ayodhya's economy, creating new opportunities, particularly in the tourism and related sectors.

In line with the vision of India's PM and UP's CM, ADA had a comprehensive plan to merge the best of India's traditions with modern infrastructure in Ayodhya. Importantly, the youth were encouraged to actively participate in this endeavour.

The competition focused on major roads such as Ram Path, Bhakti Path, Janambhoomi Path, Dharam Path, and others. The objective was to craft unique, iconic and captivating artistic expressions that would uplift the spirits of passersby and leave a lasting impact. These designs that were inspired by the Ramayana depicted the life of Shri Ram and narrated Ayodhya's history, culture, ethos and identity.

While drawing inspiration from traditional designs and the Ramayana, these murals and sculptures adopted abstract and modern artistic techniques. They adorned plain surfaces on various buildings, boundary walls and construction elements along Ayodhya's major roads. These designs were not only visible to both pedestrians and motorists but were also built to last, required low maintenance and used environment-friendly materials.

The winning designs were eventually realized on Ayodhya's major roads, attracting the attention of millions of tourists and pilgrims from around the world. The artists and designers responsible for these creations were celebrated for their significant contributions to Ayodhya's cultural heritage.

HISTORICAL AND CULTURAL SITES IN AND AROUND AYODHYA

As you prepare to embark on a soul-enriching pilgrimage to the sacred Ram Temple in Ayodhya, delve deeper into a wondrous story of heritage that complements your spiritual journey. Ayodhya, the timeless abode of Lord Ram, resonates with the divine echoes of the Ramayana. While the Ram Temple stands as the zenith of devotion, Ayodhya's landscape is adorned with a myriad of sites that enrich your experience. These gems, nestled along the banks of the Sarayu River and scattered through its winding lanes, offer a glimpse into a world where history, faith and culture converge seamlessly. Explore the enchanting mosaic that Ayodhya weaves, where every stone tells a story and every temple echoes with the legends of gods and emperors. To celebrate Ayodhya's rich heritage that complements your pilgrimage to the Ram Temple, consider exploring the following destinations in the sacred city.

Sarayu River

The river holds a significant place in the state and is mentioned in ancient Hindu texts like the Vedas and Ramayana. Its name, which translates to 'that which is streaming', perfectly encapsulates its essence. Flowing through Ayodhya, this river is considered not only a physical presence but also a spiritual one. It is believed to possess the power to rejuvenate and purify the religious town of Ayodhya. As a result, hundreds of devout pilgrims visit its banks to take a sacred dip throughout the year, especially during various religious occasions, seeking spiritual cleansing and blessings.

Hanumangarhi

Hanumangarhi stands as a venerable testament to devotion. This tenth-century temple is a sanctuary dedicated to the mighty deity, Hanuman, a beloved figure in Hindu scriptures.

Among Ayodhya's sacred sites, Hanumangarhi occupies a place of profound significance. The temple, atop a hill, boasts a staircase of 76 steps. Upon reaching the top, a breathtaking panorama of rolling hills unfolds, cradling the temple in their protective embrace. Here, in this ethereal abode, resides a diminutive 6-inch idol of Hanuman, a symbol of boundless strength in humble guise. The temple's inner sanctum, nestled within a natural cave, bears witness to a splendid array of Hanuman's incarnations. The divine presence is not solitary; it's accompanied by the benevolent figure of Maa Anjani, Hanuman's mother. During the vibrant celebrations of Ram Navami and Hanuman Jayanti, this sacred site comes alive with the fervour of thousands of devotees. (Ram Navami honours the birth of Lord Ram, while Hanuman Jayanti reverberates with celebration for the birth of Lord Hanuman.) These occasions transform Hanumangarhi into a vibrant hub of spiritual awakening, drawing pilgrims from far and wide to bask in the divine aura of Hanuman's grace.[35]

Kanak Bhawan (The Golden House)

In the serene realm of Tulsi Nagar, in the northeastern embrace of Ram Janmabhoomi, stands the enchanting Kanak Bhawan. This sacred abode constructed in 1891, often referred to as the 'Golden Palace', is a testament to devotion, dedicated to the divine couple, Lord Ram and Goddess Sita. The sanctum sanctorum of the temple shelters resplendent idols, their golden crowns glistening beneath a silver canopy. Legend has it that this shrine was a generous gift from Kaikeyi, Lord Ram's stepmother, to the divine couple.

Over the course of history, during the reign of Vikramaditya, the temple underwent a meticulously designed renovation. However, its most striking transformation was orchestrated by the visionary Vrishbhanu Kunwari in 1891, giving rise to the Bundela-style architectural marvel that we behold today. Presently, the custodianship of this sacred haven rests with the Sri Vrishbhan Dharma Setu Trust, ensuring its continued grace and spiritual significance.

Shri Nageshwarnath Temple

Standing proudly beside the bustling Theri Bazaar in Ayodhya is the Nageshwarnath Temple, dedicated to the revered deity, Lord Nageshwarnath. This sacred haven is steeped in history, believed to have been founded by Kusha, the son of Lord Rama.

While the temple's roots trace back to the year 750 CE, the present structure as we know it was meticulously reconstructed in 1750. This ambitious endeavour was spearheaded by Naval Rai, the sagacious minister of Safar Jung. Legend weaves an enchanting tale that led to the temple's creation: Kusha, in a twist of fate, lost his precious arm ring in the local bath. Little did he know that this would set in motion a profound connection. He encountered a Nag Kanya (a girl from the Nag tribe), a fervent devotee of Lord Shiva, and their destinies intertwined. In gratitude for her love and devotion, Kusha, with a heart brimming with reverence, erected this Shaiva temple, dedicating it to the Nag Kanya. Today, the Nageshwarnath Temple stands as a testimony to their divine union and continues to draw devotees from far and wide. The temple's spiritual aura is particularly vibrant during the auspicious occasions of Mahashivaratri and Trayodashi, also known as Pradosh Vrat or Pradosh Vratam, celebrated with great fervour. One of its grand highlights is the Shiva Barat, a majestic procession that honours Lord Shiva, enthralling all who witness it.

Sita Ki Rasoi

Located on the northwestern side of Ayodhya's Rajkot, adjacent to the Ram Janmabhoomi, lies a place steeped in divinity and history—Sita Ki Rasoi. This sacred site is believed to be the ancient kitchen used by Goddess Sita herself during her time in Ayodhya. Today, it has been transformed into a temple, housing a collection of historic vessels. Sita Ki Rasoi is one of the two revered kitchens dedicated to Sita's name, and it stands as a testament to her connection with the culinary arts. This unique temple features a basement kitchen, providing a glimpse into the daily life of the Goddess. On the opposite end of the temple, you'll find elaborately adorned idols of Lord Ram, Lakshman, Bharat, Shatrughan and their respective consorts—Sita, Urmila, Mandavi and Srutakirti. In keeping with its tradition, the temple offers free meals to visitors, and donations for charitable causes are also accepted with an open heart. Sita Ki Rasoi is not only a place of devotion but also a symbol of the deep-rooted cultural and culinary heritage associated with Ramayana.

Treta Ke Thakur Temple

Perched serenely along Ayodhya's Naya Ghat, the Treta Ke Thakur Temple is a sacred abode hosting a pantheon of revered idols, including Lord Ram, Sita, Lakshman, Hanuman, Bharat and Sugreev. These intricate statues, all meticulously carved from a single black sandstone, add to the temple's historical and spiritual significance. The temple's origins can be traced back 300 years, a testimony to its enduring importance.

Legend has it that it stands on the very ground where Lord Ram performed his grand Ashwamedha Yagna. In the 1700s, during the reign of the Maratha queen Ahilyabai Holkar, the temple underwent significant restoration, preserving its architectural and religious heritage. Interestingly, the Treta Ke Thakur Temple opens its doors to the public just once a year, specifically on the auspicious occasion of Ekadashi. This sacred day falls on the eleventh day of the Shukla Paksha during the month of Kartik in the Hindu calendar. During this annual event, vibrant and culturally rich celebrations take place, allowing devotees to partake in cherished traditions and bask in the temple's divine aura.

Birla Temple

Standing proudly as a testament to devotion, the Shri Ram Janaki Birla Temple graces Ayodhya as a newly constructed sanctuary of faith. This sacred abode is strategically situated opposite the Ayodhya Bus Station along the Ayodhya–Faizabad route, making it accessible to all who seek the divine presence. The temple pays homage to the revered Lord Ram and the divine Goddess Sita. As visitors approach, they are greeted by the temple's resplendent aura, where the spiritual resonance of the deities is palpable. This sacred haven offers a place of solace and reverence for pilgrims and devotees who journey to Ayodhya.

Tulsi Smarak Bhawan

On the eastern outskirts of Ayodhya, precisely at the Rajganj Crossing along the National Highway, lies the enchanting Tulsi Smarak or the Ramcharitmanas Smarak. This magnificent tribute to Lord Ram's epic journey through the pages of the Ramcharitmanas was erected in 1969 under the visionary leadership of Shri Vishwanath Das, the then governor of UP. The heart of this splendid edifice is its expansive library, a veritable treasure trove brimming with a wealth of literary gems. But that's not all; the Tulsi Smarak also harbours the esteemed 'Ayodhya Research Sansthan', a centre dedicated to unravelling the profound cultural, spiritual and literary dimensions of Ayodhya. You'll be captivated by the vibrant Ramayana artistry and craftsmanship on display, a true feast for the senses. To keep the spirit of Ramayana alive, the centre resonates with the daily recitation of Ram Katha. In 1988, a splendid addition came to grace this revered complex—the Ram Katha Sanghralaya, a museum that serves as a custodian of an extensive collection of historical treasures, including invaluable artifacts, facts and data, all meticulously chronicling the life and era of Lord Shri Ram. As the sun sets over Ayodhya, the Tulsi Smarak comes to life with melodious devotional songs, inspiring sermons and heartfelt prayers. And when the auspicious day of Tulsi Jayanti arrives, falling on the seventh day of the Shravan month, the entire complex bursts into a grand celebration, where devotion and festivity harmoniously blend.

Dashrath Bhavan

In the heart of Ramkot Ayodhya, stands the illustrious Dashrath Bhavan, the original residence of King Dashrath, the ruler of Ayodhya and the father of Lord Ram. Often referred to as Bada Asthan or Badi Jagah, this regal palace is a place of great historical significance, housing magnificent shrines dedicated to King Ram. Dashrath Mahal is not only believed to be the abode of Lord Ram during his formative years but also served as the capital of King Dashrath. This palace boasts an ornate entrance adorned with exquisite paintings that depict tales of yore. Within its halls, one can often encounter saffron-clad monks engrossed in the chanting of mantras, melodious singing and graceful dancing, creating an ambience of spiritual serenity. While Dashrath Bhavan may be relatively smaller in scale compared to some grand palaces, it exudes an undeniable magnetic charm, particularly during festivals like Ram Vivah, Karthik Mela, Diwali, Ram Navami and Shravan Mela.

Ramkot

Perched majestically atop a serene hill, the Ramkot Temple reigns as the paramount place of devotion in Ayodhya. With its roots delving deep into antiquity, this ancient citadel rests upon an elevated platform, and local legend ascribes it as the ground where Lord Ram once held his fort. The temple comes alive with a number of vibrant cultural programmes dedicated to Lord Ram. One of the temple's most enchanting features is its panoramic vista. From this vantage point, you'll be treated to sweeping views that encompass the entire city, a bird's eye perspective of its splendid temples and the picturesque ghats along the river. Lord Hanuman himself safeguarded this citadel from within a concealed cave, enhancing the temple's aura of divinity.[36]

Mani Parvat

Mani Parvat is a small hillock located in Kami Ganj, Ayodhya. This site holds immense religious significance and is a must-visit among the religious places in Ayodhya. Mani Parvat sits at an elevation of about 65 ft above sea level, and its importance is deeply rooted in the Ramayana. According to this epic, Lord Hanuman once uprooted an entire mountain to obtain the life-reviving Sanjeevani herb, which was used to heal the wounded Lakshman after his battle with Meghnath. It is believed that a portion of this mountain fell in Ayodhya, forming the sacred site known as Mani Parbat. This hillock is closely situated next to another mound called Sugreev Parbat.

Legend has it that Lord Buddha spent six years in Ayodhya and delivered his sermons on the Law of Dharma from Mani Parbat. Additionally, the hillock is adorned with a stupa, believed to have been built by Emperor Ashoka, as well as a Buddhist monastery. The pinnacle of Mani Parvat offers a breathtaking panoramic view of Ayodhya and its surrounding landscapes.

Swarg Dwar

Swarg Dwar, also known as Ram Ghat, stands gracefully half a kilometer to the north of the Ram Janmabhoomi in Ayodhya. The significance of bathing on this ghat is deeply rooted in Indian mythology. As one approaches the sacred banks of the river, a sense of reverence washes over them. This strip of land, stretching from Sahasradhara to the Nageshwarnath Temple, is often referred to as Swarg Dwar—the gateway to heaven. It's a place where history and spirituality converge. The riverfront at Swarg Dwar, thus makes one feel the past, where Rama's journey on this earthly realm met its poignant conclusion.

Ram Ki Paidi

Ram Ki Paidi is a collection of steps leading down to the banks of the holy Sarayu River. Ram Ki Paidi is essentially a flight of steps situated on Nayaghat, near the Sarayu River's edge, where a vast number of pilgrims and devotees come to take ritual bath in the sacred waters of the river. The original steps were swept away by the powerful currents of the river. However, a new ghat with steps was constructed between 1984 and 1985.

Surrounding the ghats, one finds lush green gardens and a cluster of temples. The riverfront presents a majestic panorama, especially when illuminated at night. Ram Ki Paidi witnesses large gatherings of devotees during festivals dedicated to Lord Ram. One of the grandest events in Ayodhya, Deepotsav, is celebrated at Ram Ki Paidi during Diwali every year.

Sita Kund

Sita Kund, located in the Kami Ganj region and in close proximity to the sacred Sarayu River, holds profound significance as one of the holiest sites in this revered city. It is said that just as Lord Ram would take daily bath at Swarg Dwar, Goddess Sita would take her daily bath in this reservoir called Sita Kund. This sacred site finds mention in the Ayodhya Mahatmya section of the Skanda Purana, where Sage Agastya reveals its precise location—to the west of the Tilodaki–Sarayu sangam, a geographical feature that remains true to this day. The site is known to fulfil the deepest desires of devotees. Surprisingly, this site remains relatively untouched by the bustling crowds of pilgrims, offering a serene and contemplative sanctuary for those seeking a profound spiritual connection.

Surya Kund

A tranquil oasis that whispers tales of a bygone era is the Surya Kund. This splendid creation, adorned with elegant

ghats, was crafted with unwavering devotion by the illustrious
rulers of Suryavansh, the solar dynasty of Ayodhya, as a
splendid homage to the radiant Sun God. Surya Kund invites
you to linger by its shores, basking in the gentle embrace of
the sun's warm rays. It's a place where you can lose yourself
in contemplation, where the worries of the world seem to
fade into the background.

Guptar Ghat

Guptar Ghat is a sacred ghat situated on the banks of the revered
Sarayu River near Ayodhya. According to legend, it is believed
to be the very spot where Lord Ram engaged in meditation
and performed Jal Samadhi, a ritual involving immersion in
water, to return to his heavenly abode 'Vaikuntha'. Devotees
flock to this ghat with the belief that taking a holy dip in the
Sarayu River at Guptar Ghat will cleanse them of their sins
and free them from worldly anxieties. The atmosphere here
resonates with the melodious chants of Lord Ram's name as
devotees and priests sing hymns in his praise.

In the past, Guptar Ghat was in close proximity to the
colonial-era Company Gardens, now known as the Guptar
Ghat Van. Among the various temples gracing this area, the
Sita–Ram temple, Chakrahari shrine and the Narsingh temple
are particularly popular. The ghat underwent significant
renovation during the 1800s and has been continually
upgraded by the state government, now equipped with
modern amenities to cater to the needs of visitors.

Makhaudha Dham

Makhaudha Dham, situated on the northern bank of the river
Sarayu, holds great historical and religious significance. It is

believed to be the site where Lord Dashrath, the father of
Lord Ram, conducted the Putra-Kameshthi yagna (ritual for
the desire of children). At this location, one would find a small
temple and the surrounding structures that commemorate
this ancient yagna, said to have taken place during the Treta
Yuga. King Dashratha had entrusted sage Rishyasringa with
the responsibility of performing this sacred ritual. The nearby
area also contains the ashram of Sage Rishyasringa, known
as Shringinari, adding to the spiritual heritage of the region.

Nandigram, Uttar Pradesh

Nandigram, historically known as Bharatkund, is a village
with deep religious significance located in the Sohawal tehsil
of Ayodhya district in the Indian state of UP. During Lord
Ram's exile, King Bharat ruled from Nandigram instead
of the kingdom's capital, Ayodhya. Nandigram is situated
approximately 19 km (12 miles) to the south of Ayodhya
city, which serves as the district headquarters.

Ram Van Gaman Path

In the pursuit of connecting with the divine, it is often said
that one should follow the footsteps of their beloved deity
by heart and with all honesty to lead a righteous life. In an
extraordinary manifestation of this profound sentiment, even
in the era of Kali Yuga, devotees find themselves blessed
to trace the path of their Lord not just psychologically but
physically. In the case of Lord Rama, this is made possible
through the Ram Van Gaman Path. This sacred route mirrors
the very path that Lord Ram walked during his 14-year exile.
It allows us to not only to follow in his physical footsteps
but also to emulate the ideals of Lord Ram within our hearts

as we not only witness but also become part of the various depictions and stories woven around each place, immersing ourselves in the rich tapestry of his divine journey. This path unites us with the living legend of the Ramayana in a tangible way.

The Ram Van Gaman Path route that echoes with the footfalls of Shri Ram, Mata Sita and Shri Lakshman begins in Ayodhya and concludes in Sri Lanka. Following their departure from Ayodhya, the three embarked on a journey through the dense woodlands spanning across what are now the states of UP, Jharkhand, Chhattisgarh, Madhya Pradesh, Odisha, Karnataka, Maharashtra and Tamil Nadu. The state governments of Chattisgrah, Madhya Pradesh and UP plan to retrace the Ram Van Gaman Marg by developing the path on the lines of Shri Ram's journey of exile. In UP, specifically, where a 177 km section of road has been in development, the proposed route will connect Ayodhya to Chitrakoot via Faizabad, Sultanpur, Pratapgarh, Jethwara, Shringverpur, Manjhanpur and Rajapur.

For the curious traveller with an adventurous heart and a thirst for divine connection, this path is a gateway to the legend of legends, a chance to immerse yourself in the epic saga of Lord Ram. When embarking on a mystical journey that traces the footsteps of Lord Ram, a voyage through time and spirituality known as the Ram Van Gaman Path, a devotee can imagine walking the very route that Lord Ram, along with his devoted wife Sita and loyal brother Lakshman, once traversed during their years of exile. One could step onto the sacred ground where stories of valour and righteousness have echoed through the ages. The Ram Van Gaman Path is a story woven with the threads of mythology and history, where every stone, every tree and every whispering breeze is said to resonate with the divine.

As one follows this sacred trail, they'll encounter ancient shrines, serene riversides and lush forests that have stood as silent witnesses to Lord Ram's noble quest—the picturesque Chitrakoot where this holy trinity sought refuge during their exile, or the serene beauty of Panchavati where Sita was abducted, or Ramtek, where the Lord rested.

The Ram Van Gaman Path isn't just a physical journey; it's a spiritual odyssey. It's a chance to connect with the divine and experience the timeless tales of Lord Ram and his unwavering devotion to dharma (righteousness). So, a traveller seeking not just destinations but spiritual revelations may find that embarking on this extraordinary pilgrimage and letting the legend of Lord Ram guide the way, can be an enriching experience.

AYODHYA BEYOND THE RAMAYANA: A MULTIFACETED HERITAGE OF FAITH

Within the timeless folds of Ayodhya lies a rich mosaic of history, culture and architectural marvels that transcend the legends of Lord Ram. Ayodhya unveils its lesser-explored yet enchanting treasures. From the grandeur of architecture that whispers tales of emperors to ancient Buddhist sites that echo with the serenity of enlightenment, from Jain shrines that radiate spirituality to ornate temples that stand as testaments to diverse faiths, Ayodhya's cultural richness extends even beyond the country's borders, reaching as far as South Korea. Following are the mentions of such sites that dictate Ayodhya's diverse heritage over centuries.

Jain Temple and Shrines of Ayodhya: Digambar Jain Temple

Ayodhya is not only renowned as the birthplace of Lord Ram but also holds immense significance for the Jain community. This holy town is believed to be the birthplace of five Jain Tirthankaras, revered spiritual leaders. Ayodhya is adorned with numerous Jain temples, each dedicated to one of these Tirthankaras. These sacred places of worship are spread throughout the town, offering pilgrims a chance to connect with their faith. Some of these temples include the Lord Adinath Temple located near Swargdwar, the Lord Anantnath Temple at Gola Ghat, the Lord Sumantnath shrine at Ramkot, the Lord Ajitnath Temple near Saptsagar and the Lord Abhinandannath Temple in the Sarai locality. Notably, a grand Jain temple, Shri Rishabhdev Digammbar Jain Mandir stands in the Raiganj area of Ayodhya, housing an impressive 21-ft-tall idol of Lord Adinath (Rishabhdevji), the first Tirthankara in Jainism. This temple serves as a place of deep spiritual significance for Jain devotees and adds to the town's rich religious heritage.

Buddhist Temples

Buddhist relics offer a unique glimpse into Ayodhya's multicultural past. Among them, Saket stands out as an ancient Buddhist site, believed to be the birthplace of Aryadeva, a renowned Buddhist monk and philosopher. The remains of stupas and structures in the Saket complex bear witness to its once-thriving Buddhist community. Additionally, Kanak Bhawan, celebrated as a Hindu temple dedicated to Lord Ram and Goddess Sita, shares historical connections with

Buddhism, as Sita hailed from the Buddhist-rich region of Mithila. Kuber Tila, another noteworthy site, encompasses an ancient mound believed to conceal a Buddhist stupa's remnants. Ayodhya's archaeological excavations have also unearthed various Buddhist relics, underscoring the city's rich and diverse cultural history. While Ayodhya is most renowned for its association with Lord Ram, these Buddhist sites add layers of historical significance for visitors interested in exploring the city's multifaceted heritage.

Queen Heo Memorial Park

Along the banks of the River Sarayu, stands the Queen Heo Memorial Park, a tribute to an Indian princess who became a queen in a distant land. The park is a testament to a remarkable historical connection between India and South Korea. Honouring this incredible historical connection between the geographically far off, but culturally close lands, the park was inaugurated during the Deepotsav 2022 celebrations on the eve of Diwali, graced by the presence of a high-level South Korean delegation and UP CM Yogi Adityanath.

The central theme of the memorial park revolves around the extraordinary journey of Princess Suriratna, born in Ayodhya as the daughter of King Padmasen and Indumati. King Padmasen ruled over the kingdom of Kosala. At the age of 16, Princess Suriratna embarked on a transformative voyage to Korea in 48 BCE, where she wed King Kim Suro, the founder and ruler of Geumgwan Gaya, a kingdom situated in southeastern Korea. This union marked the inception of the Karak dynasty in Korea and established Princess Suriratna as Queen Heo Hwang-ok. Her arrival in Korea marked a

significant historical event, as she became the first queen of
Geumgwan Gaya, believed to be located near modern-day
Gimhae city in southern Gyeonsang province.

The legacy of Queen Heo Hwang-ok continues to endure
through the descendants of her lineage in South Korea. The
tale of her epic journey and the founding of the Karak dynasty
is recounted in various historical texts and is an integral part of
South Korean folklore. The Queen Heo Memorial Park seeks to
honour this incredible historical connection between Ayodhya
and South Korea. It features statues of Queen Heo Hwang-ok
and King Kim Suro, placed in the southeast and northeast
corners of the memorial, respectively. A picturesque pond
with a footbridge adds to the park's charm, while a striking
granite egg sculpture serving as a symbol of the golden egg
received by Princess Suriratna during her sea voyage to Korea.

SACROSANCT SPOTS IN THE VICINITY OF AYODHYA AND BEYOND

Beyond the sacred soil of Ayodhya, the legacy of Lord Ram
and the enchanting tales of the Ramayana unfurl across the
Indian subcontinent. These divine spots, etched into the
tapestry of our nation's history, beckon pilgrims and seekers
of spiritual solace to embark on a profound journey. Beyond
the resplendent Shri Ram Temple, the Ramayana extends
its benevolent hand to diverse corners of India, weaving a
celestial narrative that traverses forests, rivers and mountains.
As one treads this path of devotion, they discover the
chapters of Lord Ram's epic journey in the landscapes of
Ayodhya and far beyond, unifying the heart and soul of this
incredible nation.

Shrigverpur, UP

Situated 45 km away from Prayagraj, Shringverpur finds its mention in the epic Ramayana as the capital of the kingdom ruled by Nishadraj, often referred to as the 'King of Fishermen'. According to the legend, it was at Shringverpur that Lord Ram, accompanied by Sita and Lakshman, crossed the mighty Ganges during their journey into exile. When visiting this historically significant location, one must not miss the opportunity to explore the Sringi Rishi temple, which adds to the cultural and spiritual richness of the area.

Bhardwaj Ashram, UP

Prayagraj, an ancient city steeped in spirituality, boasts a profound connection to Shri Ram, the Ramayana and the sage Bharadwaja Brahmarshi, renowned for his wisdom. Bharadwaja Brahmarshi, one of the seven sages of Kali Yuga, is revered as the embodiment of Vedic knowledge. His texts, ahead of their time, continue to perplex experts in various fields, from science to architecture. Bharadwaja Brahmarshi's ashram is believed to have graced the banks of the sacred Ganges. It resembled a heavenly garden, teeming with fragrant flora, fruits, diverse wildlife and disciples committed to dharma, meditation, charity and penance.

It was here that Lord Ram, Sita and Lakshman encountered the sage at the outset of their exile. Bharadwaja imparted profound insights on life's purpose and directed Ram to Chitrakoot. After his triumph in Lanka, Lord Ram paid homage to Bharadwaja Rishi in his ashram and prayed to the Shivalinga, known as Bharadwajeshwar. It is said that the celestial Pushpaka Vimana was crafted in this ashram by the venerable sage.

The temple complex houses Rama's padukas and ancient idols dating back to the eighth century BCE. Rare sculptures of deities, sages and celestial beings grace the premises. Bharat Kund, Parvati Kund, Sita Kund and various smaller shrines add to the sacred aura. In 2019, a monumental statue of Bharadwaja Rishi was unveiled during the Kumbha Mela, with plans for a state-of-the-art Pushpaka Vimana installation by 2025.

Sita Samahit Sthal, UP

Sita Samahit Sthal is a revered Hindu temple located in UP's Bhadoi district, approximately 54 km from Prayagraj and 44 km from Varanasi. This temple holds both mythical and historical significance, as it is believed to be the place where Goddess Sita descended into the earth. The temple also features a remarkable 110-ft-high statue of Lord Hanuman, adding to its allure. Additionally, the temple is surrounded by a picturesque pond that further enhances its appeal, attracting numerous tourists and pilgrims.

Sitamarhi, Bihar

Sitamarhi, located in the Mithila region of Bihar is a city and the district headquarters of Sitamarhi district. It is renowned as the birthplace of Goddess Sita. The city is home to a temple dedicated to her. Additionally, Sitamarhi features a rock-cut sanctuary from the Mauryan period.

Ram Navami, a spring festival celebrated in Dumra, is a major event in Sitamarhi, marked by a grand fair. The Janaki Mandir or Janaki Sthan, a temple named after the other name of Goddess Sita with a history dating back to

1599, hosts an annual marriage ceremony re-enacting the wedding of Ram and Sita. Another important festival in Sitamarhi is Sama Chakeva, a winter celebration that honours brother–sister relationships. This cultural event includes marriage ceremonies and various rituals, requiring extensive preparation.

Chitrakoot, Madhya Pradesh

Chitrakoot, often referred to as 'the hill of many wonders', is a town located on the banks of the Mandakini River, nestled between the states of Madhya Pradesh and UP. This sacred place is believed to be the dwelling of the holy trinity of Hinduism, consisting of Lord Brahma, Lord Vishnu and Lord Shiva. According to ancient scriptures, Lord Ram, along with his wife Sita and brother Lakshman, sought refuge in the forests of Chitrakoot during their 14-year exile from the kingdom of Ayodhya. They spent 12 of those years in the serene woods, which were also inhabited by many hermits. Lakshman is said to have constructed a cottage atop a hill, known as Param Kutir, where the trio resided during their stay. Today, in place of the original wooden structure, there's a domed shrine with a pillared verandah at the site of Param Kutir. Kamadgiri Hill, situated in the southern part of Chitrakoot, holds immense spiritual significance. It is considered one of the holiest places in Chitrakoot Dham. Legend has it that Lord Brahma conducted the first yagna at this spot before the creation of life. Pilgrims follow a walking path at the base of the hill to seek the divine blessings of Lord Kamadnath, who is known as the fulfiller of wishes.

The caves at Gupt Godavari are said to have been the dwelling place of Rama, Sita and Lakshman for many years.

According to the Puranas, these caves were created by the Devas in advance, foreseeing that Ram would reside here during the Treta Yuga. The higher cave can only be accessed through a narrow passage that accommodates a single person at a time. It leads to a spacious cavern and a springwater pool known as Dhanushkund. The entrance to a lower cave is located outside this cave. Ram Ghats, bordering the Mandakini River, are believed to have been the preferred bathing spot of Ram, Sita and Lakshman. Devotees gather here every morning to perform *suryanamaskar*, a salutation to the sun, and throughout the day, the ghats are alive with religious activities, chants and the fragrance of incense. In the evening, as the sun sets, devotees return to perform aarti and offer flowers.

The Hanuman Dhara hill is adorned with shrines dedicated to Hanuman, which can be seen from the base of the hill, along the route in small pavilions, and even carved into the rocks. These shrines are vibrant in their orange hues. At Janaki Kund, one may encounter a scholar reading the Ramayana in the local dialect, Khari Boli, at a nearby pavilion situated on the banks of the Mandakini. This spot is believed to have been a private bathing area for Sita, also known as Janaki, the daughter of King Janak of Mithila.

Panchvati, Nashik, Maharashtra

In the dense Dandakaranya forests of Panchavati, situated on the banks of the sacred Godavari River, Lord Ram, Sita and Lakshman took refuge after leaving Chitrakoot during their exile. The name 'Nashik' is believed to be derived from the Sanskrit word 'Nasika', meaning nose, as this is where Lakshman famously cut off Soorpnakha's nose. It was in

Panchavati that Ravan's sister, Soorpnakha, first saw Lord Ram and fell in love with him. Her attempts to lure Ram and Lakshman failed which frustrated her. She attempted to harm Sita in retaliation, leading to Lakshman cutting off her nose as a lesson.[37] This location also marks where Mareecha, in the form of a golden deer, deceived Goddess Sita, aiding Ravana in her abduction. Panchavati holds significance in the entire episode of Sita's abduction. Various places that can be visited in Panchvati are Ram Kund, Sita Gufa, Kala Ram Mandir and Kapaleshwar Mahadev temple.

Ramtek, Maharashtra

Ramtek, situated approximately 40 km northeast of Nagpur, is traditionally believed to be a location where Lord Ram spent a portion of his exile, along with his wife, Sita and brother Lakshman.[38] The name 'Ramtek' can be interpreted in two ways. It may refer to Shri Ram of Ayodhya taking a *tek* or a vow here, pledging to rid the earth of *asura*s. Alternatively, it signifies the place where Lord Ram rested briefly during his southward journey. In the past, this hill was known as 'Tapogiri,' signifying a hill where numerous sages engaged in *tapa* or deep meditation.[39] The site is characterized by a collection of around 10 temples, some dating back to the fourth to sixth century CE. These temples are situated atop the Hill of Ram and are often inhabited by playful langur monkeys, adding to the charm of the place.

Turturiya, Chattisgrah

Turturiya is a charming village nestled within lush forests, located in the Balodabazar district of Chhattisgarh. This tranquil place boasts significant historical and religious importance.

It is believed that the renowned sage Valmiki, the author of the iconic Hindu epic Ramayana, once had his ashram here. Moreover, Turturiya is known as the birthplace of Lord Ram and Mata Sita's twin sons, Luv and Kush. The village's unique name is derived from the sound 'tur-tur' produced by the Balbhadri drain as it strikes the rocks along its course.[40]

Turturiya offers several notable attractions, including Buddhist ruins featuring intricately carved pillars and stupas constructed with bricks. Additionally, you can find distinctive idols of Lord Vishnu and Lord Ganesha here. Surrounding this village is a picturesque natural landscape that enhances its allure. Turturiya hosts a grand festival every year, celebrated from Vaishakh Poornima to Amavasya, falling roughly in May, drawing visitors to partake in its cultural and religious festivities.

Janakpur, Nepal

Janakpur, a city steeped in the ancient legends of the Ramayana, welcomes pilgrims and tourists with its vibrant festivities, pleasant climate and stunning temples. The city's rich culture rooted in Indian heritage, once thrived as the capital of the Mithila kingdom, known today for its Maithili-speaking inhabitants and renowned for its vividly colourful paintings. Janakpur's history is intertwined with the mythological discovery of baby Sita by King Janak and her life growing up leading to the divine marriage with Lord Ram. This city, which witnessed the presence of great sages like Vardhamana Mahavira and Gautama Buddha during the Mauryan Empire, remained a spiritual centre for over two millennia. In Janakpur, several places hold immense cultural and spiritual significance. Janaki Mandir, where a golden statue of Goddess Sita was found, is beautifully illuminated during early mornings. Ram Mandir, nearby, hosts special rituals during Ram Navami and Vivah Panchami. Gangasagar Pond offers serene prayers on its banks. Swargadwari, once a cemetery, is now a picturesque park with a small Hindu temple. Dhanushadham, 13 km away, has connections to the Ramayana. A Nari Bikas Kendra, a centre that empowers women showcases local art. Lastly, Mani Mandap, the original wedding site of Lord Ram and Goddess Sita, sits amidst nature.[41]

ONCE AGAIN, HIS ABODE

Ayodhya is not just a city of legends and mythology; it is a story woven with threads of history, faith and culture. Beyond its iconic Ram Temple, Ayodhya boasts a treasure trove of sacred destinations, each with its own unique significance and stories to tell. From the temples dedicated to Lord Hanuman, Lord Shiva and Lord Ram to the serene riverbanks and ancient hillocks, Ayodhya's spiritual aura is palpable and enchanting.

While Ayodhya stands as the epicentre of Lord Ram's legend, it also embraces a rich tapestry of Buddhist relics and the enduring legacy of Buddhism, as evidenced by archaeological sites and connections to Buddhist philosophers. It also celebrates the rich history of Jainism, with temples dedicated to revered Tirthankaras. Additionally, the town has forged international bonds with South Korea, celebrating the remarkable journey of Queen Heo Hwang-ok, who left Ayodhya to become a beloved queen in a distant land. Ayodhya, a land steeped in religious and cultural significance reflecting its multifaceted cultural heritage, is thus a treasure trove of history and spirituality.

Lord Ram's narrative extends across the Indian subcontinent, weaving a celestial tale that traverses forests, rivers and mountains. As one treads the path of devotion, one can encounter various spots, each laden with historical and spiritual significance. These places, connected by the threads of the Ramayana, unify the heart and soul of our incredible nation. As one leaves Ayodhya to explore these sacred sites, one notices that the journey isn't just about geographical distances; it's a spiritual odyssey. One can follow in the footsteps of Lord Ram, Mata Sita and Shri Lakshman as one immerses oneself in their timeless stories of valour, righteousness and devotion. Each place a devotee visits, unveils a chapter of this divine saga, connecting the devotee with the living legend of the Ramayana in a tangible and meaningful way.

As one embarks on this soul-enriching pilgrimage to the sacred Ram Temple in Ayodhya, one must take the time to explore the above-mentioned gems that can complement the spiritual journey. Ayodhya is a living testament to the confluence of diverse cultures, religions and histories, and it invites all to delve deeper into its multifaceted heritage, where every stone tells a story, and every temple echoes with the legends of gods and emperors. In Ayodhya, history, faith and culture converge seamlessly, offering a profound and enriching experience for all who visit. The aura of devotion and spirituality envelops them, making it a memorable destination for pilgrims and tourists alike.

CONCLUSION
The Return of Ram Lalla

'*Ram Lalla Hum Aayenge, Mandir Wahin Banayenge* (Ram Lalla, we shall arrive; the temple, we shall raise)' was not just a slogan attached with the Ayodhya Movement. It represented the aspirations of millions of Hindus, not only in India but across the world. Now, after the historic judgment by the Supreme Court of India has paved the way for the construction of the Ram Temple, Ram Lalla is set to return to his janmabhoomi. The five-century-old struggle of the Hindus has finally seen success.

There are interesting parallels to be seen in the life of Lord Ram and the culmination of the Hindu struggle in the construction of the Ram Temple. Just as Lord Ram was sentenced to a *vanvaas* or exile and was banished out of Ayodhya for 14 years, the city of Ayodhya too was without a temple of the revered Lord for over five centuries. Just as the return of Lord Ram to Ayodhya ushered in a feeling of happiness, so did the developments in the twenty-first century that finally paved the way for construction of a Ram Temple.

The reconstruction of Shri Ram Janmabhoomi Temple at

Ayodhya is of immense significance not just for Hindus and India, but beyond national and religious borders as well. Its reconstruction is different from any other monument in terms of its powerful symbolism of faith, unity and civilizational heritage. The temple is also a symbol of the hope for spiritual awakening of the coming generations.

The construction of the Ram Temple not only symbolizes resurgence of the Sanatan Dharma but of the Indian nation as a whole. Every single brick that reached the temple over the years has been dipped in faith and fired in aspirations of a new India. Set to be open on 22 January 2024, it will signify a momentous chapter of Indian history culminating after more than four centuries of struggle and perseverance. The baton of this struggle was passed down for centuries by lakhs of faithfuls wanting to reclaim their sacred land and the temple that had fallen prey to foreign invaders.

Now that the Supreme Court verdict on Ayodhya is here, it has already proved to be a game changer for the region. Huge funding has poured in; the city has got a facelift as the banks of the river Sarayu are being redeveloped. The foundations of the Ram Temple, therefore, have already begun to lay the path for the economic revival of Ayodhya, signifying much more than just being an emotional issue for Hindus. Its reconstruction not only marks a new phase of cultural awakening but also ushers in a new wave of economic development in Ayodhya

With the reopening of the temple early in 2024, Ayodhya is all set to mark a second homecoming of Lord Shri Ram. An inalienable part of India's self-respect and pride, the Ram Janmabhoomi Temple is part of a national and civilizational rejuvenation and carries forth the universal message of Lord

Shri Ram that transcends religious barriers.

The judgment and the resultant victory for Indians has also shown to the world that complex issues can be solved through democratic and constitutional methods. The fact that there has been not even an iota of violence after the historic judgment of the Supreme Court is a testimony to the peace and mutual respect that is prevalent in the country. This peace and mutual respect is also regarded as one of the chief traits of the Ram-Rajya. It would not be futile to expect that these tenets of Ram-Rajya further develop in Indian society and lead to a more prosperous and developed country, marked by equality, mutual respect and tolerance for all.

ACKNOWLEDGEMENT

I come from the region of Awadh where Lord Shri Ram and his tales live in every house. Ramcharitmanas is a part of day-to-day life, and one grows up listening to it from elders, friends and family members. As it is for millions of others, Lord Shri Ram has been a huge part of my subconscious too. I have witnessed various developments related to Ram Janmabhoomi Temple over the years. It is a matter of great honour for me that, with the blessings of Lord Shri Ram, I got the opportunity to author this book.

I bow down to my father and grandfather for directly and indirectly guiding me in these endeavours. They are no longer in this world to witness this powerful and emotional moment but they will keep inspiring me.

I owe gratitude to Late Vireshwar Dwivedi ji, an RSS pracharak who was closely associated with the Ram Temple Movement for five decades. He was my father's friend and I spent many an hour in close association with him. His company gave me the chance to develop my understanding on the subject through him and his life's work.

Words are not enough to thank Rajendra Pankaj ji, a senior VHP leader who has been closely associated with the temple construction work. Pankaj ji shared rare insights about the Ram Temple Movement. He provided me with invaluable access and guidance and mentored me through the course of writing this book. I am also immensely grateful to Champat Rai ji. I had many opportunities over the years to interact with him, which helped me shape and refine my ideas.

Dr Meenakshi Jain's books, especially the ones on Lord Ram and Ayodhya, have been my constant companion in this process and they are a must-read for everyone. Writings of Konrad Elst, Dr David Frawley and Prof Pralay Kanungo have also been a huge inspiration. I also want to thank my team members Pawan Mathur and Smriti for providing research support.

Immense gratitude is also due to chief editor of Rupa Publications Yamini Chowdhary who showed trust in commissioning this book and to my editor Richa Tewari who devoted great rigour and energy to add value and enhance the quality of the book. I also thank the staff of the Prime Minister Museum and Library (PMML) for providing the perfect precincts for undertaking this work.

Finally, no words can do justice to my sense of gratitude towards my mother, grandmother and other family members who were perhaps the first heralds of Lord Ram in my life.

It may not be possible to include all names here but I am grateful to all who have been my companions in this journey. All the good things in this book are owed to the wonderful people in my life and all flaws are mine.

NOTES

Introduction: Await the Arrival

1   Ramcharitmanas, 1.140.5

2   Gururaj, Raghu, 'Relevance of Ramayana in Indonesia,' *Transcontinental Times*, 31 March 2021, https://tinyurl.com/4yhf67ev. Accessed on 3 November 2023.

3   'The Ramayanas of Southeast Asia', *Center for Southeast Asia and Its Diasporas, University of Washington*, https://tinyurl.com/4whjmzhw. Accessed on 3 November 2023.

4   'The Ramayana in South-East Asia: Malaysia', *Wayback Machine*, https://tinyurl.com/mbcm9j3r. Accessed on 15 November 2023.

5   Singh, Sherry-Ann, 'The Ramayana in Trinidad: A Socio-Historical Perspective,' *The Journal of Caribbean History*, Vol. 44, No. 2, 2010, www.proquest.com/docview/868179129. Accessed on 3 November 2023.

6   Bhagirat, Lakhram, 'Ramlila–An Introspective Gift from Our Ancestors', *Guyana Times*, 15 April 2019, https://tinyurl.com/3ap685fa. Accessed on 3 November 2023.

7   Sharma, Subhash, 'Ram Rajya Vision: An Analytical Perspective,' *SSRN Electronic Journal*, 13 February 2020, https://doi.org/10.2139/ssrn.3537521. Accessed on 30 April 2022.

8   Pandey, Kirti, 'Ram and Ram Rajya: For Millions of Hindus, Lord Ram Is Synonymous with an Ideal Ruler,' *Times Now News*, 5 August 2020, tinyurl.com/4zhc9s8p. Accessed 3 November 2023.

9   Shakti Shekhar, Kumar, 'Ram Temple Existed Before Babri Mosque

in Ayodhya: Archaeologist KK Muhammed' *The Times of India*, 1 October 2010, https://tinyurl.com/2hbheee9. Accessed on 10 November 2023.

10   Prasoon, Satya, 'Timeline: Key Events in the Babri Masjid–Ram Mandir Controversy', *Supreme Court Observer*, 22 October 2018, https://tinyurl.com/2mn9x9dj. Accessed on 20 August 2023.

Chapter 1: Along the Sarayu, Lies the Invincible

1   Garud Purana 2.38.5; Shastri, J.L., *Garud Purana: Ancient Indian Tradition and Mythology 12–14*, Motilal Banarsidass, Delhi, 1982.

2   'Avatars of Vishnu,' *MANAS*, University of California, https://tinyurl.com/bdarbwdv. Accessed on 6 November 2023.

3   Gopal, Lallanji (ed.), *Ayodhya, History, Archeology and Tradition*, All India Kashiraj Trust, 1994, p. 14.

4   Kishore, Kunal, *Ayodhya Revisited*, Ocean Books Pvt Limited, 2016, p. 4.

5   Kishore, Kunal, *Ayodhya Revisited*, Ocean Books Pvt Limited, 2016, p. 2.

6   'The Antiquity of Ayodhya and Its Emergence As a World-famous City', 17 August 2022, *Hindu Post*, https://tinyurl.com/5n8p2mxy. Accessed on 15 August 2023.

7   Hegade, Sandhya, 'The City Called Ayodhya', *Medium*, 7 November 2021, https://tinyurl.com/yc72run7. Accessed on 15 August 2023.

8   Mukherjee, Sutapa, *Ayodhya: Past and Present*, Harper Collins India, 2022.

9   'City of Ayodhya: Brief Historical Facts', *VHPA*, Vishwa Hindu Parishad of America, 2023, https://www.vhp-america.org/rjb/ayodhya-history/. Accessed on 30 October 2023.

10   Tarn, William Woodthorpe, *The Greeks in Bactria and India*, Cambridge University Press, 2010, pp. 452–456.

11   Kishore, Kunal, *Ayodhya Revisited*, Ocean Books Pvt Limited, 2016, p. 22.

12   Agarwal, Ashwini, *Rise and Fall of Imperial Guptas*, Motilal Banarasidas, 1989, p. 126.

13   Dube, Amarnath, 'Buddha in Ayodhya IV: Kakuda Sutta', *Medium*, 12 October 2019, https://tinyurl.com/2s4ebbmf. Accessed on 30 October 2023.

14 Pandey, Lalta Prasad, *Ayodhya: The Abode of Rama and the Dharmaksetra of Lord Buddha and the Jaina Tirthankaras*, Munshilal Manoharlal Publishers Pvt Ltd, 2009, p. 16.

15 Ibid. 35

16 Chishti, Seema, 'Long Ago, by the Sarayu', *The Indian Express*, 27 October 2019, https://tinyurl.com/yeebsm6u. Accessed on 14 August 2023.

17 Ibid.

18 Ibid.

19 Pandey, Lalta Prasad, *Ayodhya: The Abode of Rama and the Dharmaksetra of Lord Buddha and the Jaina Tirthankaras*, Munshilal Manoharlal Publishers Pvt Ltd, 2009, p. 16.

20 Dube, Amarnath, 'Ayodhya: You Must Have Heard Name', *Medium*, 6 October 2019, https://tinyurl.com/2pvc8vz4. Accessed on 14 August 2023.

21 Chavan, Akshay, 'Ayodhya: History Beyond the Epics and Politics', *Peepul Tree*, 5 August 2020, https://tinyurl.com/ycc4nhff. Accessed on 14 August 2023.

22 Ibid.

23 Kishore, Kunal, *Ayodhya Revisited*, Ocean Books Pvt Limited, 2016, p. 40.

24 Ibid. 42.

25 Pandey, Lalta Prasad, *Ayodhya: The Abode of Rama and the Dharmaksetra of Lord Buddha and the Jaina Tirthankaras*, Munshilal Manoharlal Publishers Pvt Ltd, 2009, p. 72.

26 Mahajan, V. D, *Muslim Rule in India*, S. Chand and Company, 2017, p. 28.

27 Kishore, Kunal, *Ayodhya Revisited*, Ocean Books Pvt Limited, 2016, pp. 50–53.

28 Pandey, Lalta Prasad, *Ayodhya: The Abode of Rama and the Dharmaksetra of Lord Buddha and the Jaina Tirthankaras*, Munshilal Manoharlal Publishers Pvt Ltd, 2009, p. 72.

29 Ibid. 73

30 Habib, Irfan, 'Medieval Ayodhya (Awadh), Down To The Mughal Occupation,' *Proceedings of the Indian History Congress*, Vol. 67, 2006, pp. 358–82. http://www.jstor.org/stable/44147957. Accessed on 6 November 2023.

31   Chavan, Akshay, 'Ayodhya: History Beyond the Epics and Politics',
      Peepul Tree, 5 August 2020, https://tinyurl.com/ycc4nhff. Accessed
      on 14 August 2023.

32   Vati, Lalita, 'Ayodhya in the Sultanate Period', *Ayodhya, History,
      Archeology and Tradition,* Lallanji Gopal (ed.), All India Kashiraj
      Trust, 1994, pp. 357–358.

33   Jain, Sandhya, 'Tulsidas's Testimony', *The Pioneer*, 18 August 2020,
      https://tinyurl.com/vtkjj4ar. Accessed on 6 November 2023.

34   Habib, Irfan, 'Medieval Ayodhya (Awadh), Down To The Mughal
      Occupation,' *Proceedings of the Indian History Congress*, Vol. 67, 2006,
      pp. 358–82. http://www.jstor.org/stable/44147957. Accessed on 6
      November 2023.

35   Lal, Makkhan, 'Even Akbar Built a "Chabutara" inside Babri Masjid
      for Hindus to Worship', 6 December 2017, *The Print*, https://tinyurl.
      com/y3n9zh9e. Accessed on 6 November 2023.

36   Cited by Bansal, Jai. G, 'Islamic Destruction of Hindu Temples: In
      their Own Words (16)', *Stop Hindudvesha*, 16 July 2022, https://
      tinyurl.com/4xrfpthz. Accessed on 6 November 2023.

37   Chavan, Akshay, 'Ayodhya: History Beyond the Epics and Politics',
      Peepul Tree, 5 August 2020, https://tinyurl.com/ycc4nhff. Accessed
      on 14 August 2023.

38   Saxena, B.S , 'Nawabs of Oudh and Their Secularism', *Repertoire
      On Wajid Ali Shah & Monuments of Avadh*, Avadh Cultural Club,
      Lucknow, 1974, https://tinyurl.com/2ma2bakk. Accessed on 6
      November 2023.

39   Kazmi, Sabina, 'Colonial Intervention In Awadh: Indigenous
      Political Structures And Indirect Rule In Eighteenth Century',
      Proceedings of the Indian History Congress , Vol. 74, 2013, pp.
      447–457, https://www.jstor.org/stable/44158845. Accessed on 10
      November 2023.

Chapter 2: The Long Haul

1   Jain, Meenakshi, *The Battle for Rama: Case of the Temple at Ayodhya*,
      Aryan Books International, 2017, p. 2.

2   Kishore, Kunal, *Ayodhya Revisited*, Ocean Books Pvt Limited, 2016,
      p. xxx

3   Chavan, Akshay, 'Ayodhya: History Beyond the Epics and Politics',

Peepul Tree, 5 August 2020, https://tinyurl.com/ycc4nhff. Accessed on 14 August 2023.

4   Kishore, Kunal, *Ayodhya Revisited*, Ocean Books Pvt Limited, 2016, p. xxx

5   'In the Supreme Court of India/Civil Appellate Jurisdiction/Review Petition (Civil) No. Of 2019/ In/Civil Appeal Nos. 10866-10867 Of 2010: M. Siddiq (D) Thr. Lrs v. Mahant Suresh Das & Ors. Etc. Etc.', *Live Law*, 2019, https://tinyurl.com/2pdpabd3. Accessed on 7 November 2023.

6   Jain, Meenakshi, *The Battle for Rama: Case of the Temple at Ayodhya*, Aryan Books International, 2017, p. 2.

7   'In the Supreme Court of India/Civil Appellate Jurisdiction/Review Petition (Civil) No. Of 2019/ In/Civil Appeal Nos. 10866-10867 Of 2010: M. Siddiq (D) Thr. Lrs v. Mahant Suresh Das & Ors. Etc. Etc.', *Live Law*, 2019 https://tinyurl.com/2pdpabd3. Accessed on 7 November 2023.

8   Ibid.

9   Ibid.

10   Ibid.

11   Ashraf, Ajaz, 'From 1855 to 2010: A Legal History of How the Babri Masjid in Ayodhya Was Turned into a Temple for Lord Ram', *Firstpost*, 7 December 2017, https://tinyurl.com/k8mrahc9. Accessed on 7 November 2023.

12   Ibid.

13   Jain, Meenakshi, *The Battle for Rama: Case of the Temple at Ayodhya*, Aryan Books International, 2017, pp. 59–70.

14   Kishore, Kunal, *Ayodhya Revisited*, Ocean Books Pvt Limited, 2016, p. xxxi.

15   Jain, Meenakshi, *The Battle for Rama: Case of the Temple at Ayodhya*, Aryan Books International, 2017, p. 70.

16   Ibid. 71.

17   Ibid. 71–72.

18   Ibid. 73.

19   Narain, Harsh, *The Ayodhya Temple–Mosque Dispute Focus on Muslim Sources*, Penman Publishers, 1993, pp. 6–17.

20   Ibid. 28.

21   Ibid. 29.

22 Ibid. 29.
23 Ibid. 29–30.
24 Ibid. 30–31.
25 Ibid. 35.
26 Jain, Meenakshi, *The Battle for Rama: Case of the Temple at Ayodhya*, Aryan Books International, 2017, p. 52.
27 Ibid. 19.
28 Ibid. 23.
29 Ibid. 29.
30 Ibid. 29.
31 Ibid. 30.
32 Ibid. 30.
33 'Extract from Alexander Cunningham's first journal in 1862, wherein he describes the ancient city of Ayodhya in great detail', *Rare Book Society of India*, 17 January 2013, https://tinyurl.com/3v2mf8ps. Accessed on 20 August 2023.
34 Roychaudhary, Adrija, '"Hindu Revivalism?": Why Jawaharlal Nehru Disapproved Rajendra Prasad's Presence at Somnath Temple Inauguration', *The Indian Express*, 5 August 2020, https://tinyurl.com/2tk5hkmk. Accessed on 20 August 2023.
35 Lal, Makhan, 'On KM Munshi's Birth Anniversary, Remembering His Fight to Rebuild Somnath Temple', *The Print*, 30 December 2018, https://tinyurl.com/3uexutdr. Accessed on 20 August, 2023.
36 Anand, Arun, and Vijay Nalwa, *Ramjanmabhoomi: Truth Evidence Faith*, Prabhat Prakashan, 2020. p. 51.
37 Ibid. 51.
38 Jain, Meenakshi, *The Battle for Rama: Case of the Temple at Ayodhya*, Aryan Books International, 2017, p. 52.
39 Ibid. 75.
40 Ibid. 76.
41 Anand, Arun, and Vijay Nalwa, *Ramjanmabhoomi: Truth Evidence Faith*, Prabhat Prakashan, 2020. p. 57.
42 Sharma, Hemant, *Ayodhya: A Battleground*, Rupa Publications, 2020, p. 250.
43 Ibid.
44 'Ayodhya: The Legal Wrangle', *Outlook*, 5 February 2020, https://tinyurl.com/5cmnk44k. Accessed on 20 August 2023.

45 Dwivedi, Ratnesh , 'India and Beyond What Lies Beneath : Digging The Ayodhya Facts', *Russian International Affairs Council*, 8 December 2018, https://tinyurl.com/24kr9vtx. Accessed on 8 November 2023.

46 Gupta, Jahnavi, 'Congress First Political Party to Encourage Ayodhya Movement, Says New Book,' *Hindustan Times*, 2 December 2020, https://tinyurl.com/bddeunzv. Accessed on 20 August 2023.

47 As told to the Author by VHP leader Rajendra Pankaj, who closely worked with Ashok Singhal in the Ram Temple movement and is currently associated with Ram Temple construction work, in a personal interview on 20 September 2023

48 Ibid.

49 Ibid.

50 Ibid.

51 Bharatiya Janata Party, *BJP's White Paper on Ayodhya and the Rama Temple Movement*, 1993, https://tinyurl.com/44nnx3bw. Accessed on 10 November 2023.

52 Anand, Arun, and Vijay Nalwa, *Ramjanmabhoomi: Truth Evidence Faith*, Prabhat Prakashan, 2020. p. 63.

53 Bharatiya Janata Party, *BJP's White Paper on Ayodhya and the Rama Temple Movement*, 1993, https://tinyurl.com/44nnx3bw. Accessed on 10 November 2023.

54 Ibid.

55 Sharma, Hemant, 'Jab Mulayam Singh Ne Kaha, Ayodhya Me Parinda Bhi Par Nahi Mar Sakta (When Mulayam Singh said not even a bird could flutter over Ayodhya)', *Navbharat Times*, https://tinyurl.com/n6btp56m. Accessed on 10 November 2023.

56 Dwivedi, Ratnesh, 'India and Beyond What Lies Beneath: Digging The Ayodhya Facts', *Russian International Affairs Council*, 8 December 2018, https://tinyurl.com/24kr9vtx. Accessed on 8 November 2023.

57 Anand, Arun, and Vijay Nalwa, *Ramjanmabhoomi: Truth Evidence Faith*, Prabhat Prakashan, 2020. p. 75.

58 Ibid. 76.

59 Prasoon, Satya, 'Timeline: Key Events in the Babri Masjid–Ram Mandir Controversy', *Supreme Court Observer*, 22 October 2018, https://tinyurl.com/2mn9x9dj. Accessed on 20 August 2023.

60 'Ram Temple Construction to Begin by March 2002', *The Times of*

India, 28 May 2001, https://tinyurl.com/u4erdzhk. Accessed on 30 October 2023.

Chapter 3: The Verdict

1   'Chronology of Ayodhya Land Dispute Case', *The Hindu Business Line,* 6 December 2021, https://tinyurl.com/4y4fjrtz. Accessed on 20 August 2023.

2   Venkasen V, 'The Excavation Order', *Frontline,* 28 March 2003, https://tinyurl.com/bd53tsxs. Accessed on 20 August 2023.

3   'HC Orders Excavations', *Tribune,* 6 March 2003, https://tinyurl.com/bdzey9hu. Accessed on 20 August 2023.

4   Ibid.

5   Malik, Ashok, 'Ayodhya Dispute: Digging History Is Surgical, Painstaking and Frustrating', *India Today,* 24 March 2003, https://tinyurl.com/bdcrhca6. Accessed on 23 August 2023.

6   Ahmed, Farzand, 'ASI Finds Temple Lies Below Babri Masjid, VHP Sees Prospect Of Reviving Ayodhya Campaign', *India Today,* 8 September 2003, https://tinyurl.com/58jtrms7. Accessed on 20 August 2003.

7   'Ayodhya Verdict: Allahabad High Court Says Divide Land in 3 Ways', *NDTV,* 1 October 2010, https://tinyurl.com/47mm9sej. Accessed on 20 August 2023.

8   Bindra, Japnam, 'What Was the Allahabad HC Verdict on Ram Janmabhoomi Babri Masjid Land Title Case', *Mint,* 9 November 2019, https://tinyurl.com/5cs2xbat. Accessed on 20 August 2023.

9   Venkteshan J, 'Supreme Court Stays Allahabad High Court Verdict on Ayodhya', 9 May 2011, https://tinyurl.com/43asvdrb. Accessed on 13 November 2023.

10 'Babri Masjid Demolition: A Timeline Of The Ram Janmabhoomi Dispute Case', *Outlook,* 31 August 2022, https://tinyurl.com/bdjn23w4. Accessed on 20 August 2023.

11 'Security Around Supreme Court Beefed Up Ahead Of Ayodhya Verdict', *India Today,* Updated on 4 April 2022, https://tinyurl.com/ytavxntd. Accessed on 20 August 2023.

12 Ibid.

13 'Ayodhya Verdict: Understanding the Supreme Court Judgment', *Hindustan Times,* 28 July 2020, https://tinyurl.com/4d5dzvbv.

Accessed on 20 August 2023.

14 'In the Supreme Court of India/Civil Appellate Jurisdiction/Review Petition (Civil) No. Of 2019/ In/Civil Appeal Nos. 10866-10867 Of 2010: M. Siddiq (D) Thr. Lrs v. Mahant Suresh Das & Ors. Etc. Etc.', *Live Law*, 2019 https://tinyurl.com/2pdpabd3. Accessed on 7 November 2023.

15 Sinha, Arunav, 'In Ayodhya, Devotees Rejoice at SC Verdict, Many Say They Are Relieved and Hope for Peace', 9 November 2019, *Mint*, https://tinyurl.com/58dm6bxv. Accessed on 20 August 2023.

16 PTI, 'Muslim Community Leaders Accept Ayodhya Verdict, Call for Peace', *Financial Express*, 9 November 2019, https://tinyurl.com/y995r33t. Accessed on 20 August 2023.

17 Varma, Shyalaja, 'Ayodhya Verdict: "Temple Of Justice Has Amicably Resolved Issue": PM Modi On Ayodhya Order', 9 November 2019, *NDTV*, https://tinyurl.com/58feu8wy. Accessed on 25 August 2023.

18 Prime Minister's Office, 'The Verdict of Supreme Court Marks the Start of a New Dawn', *Press Information Bureau*, 9 November 2019, https://tinyurl.com/3twwwe9n. Accessed on 25 August 2023.

19 'A Historical and Emotional Day: L.K. Advani Speaks On Ram Mandir Bhoomi Pujan', YouTube, https://tinyurl.com/32yctb7d. Accessed on 16 November 2023.

20 Ramachandran, Smriti Kak, 'Ayodhya Verdict: Supreme Court's Judgment Brought out the Truth, Says RSS', *Hindustan Times*, 9 November 2019, https://tinyurl.com/3w3ty9x4. Accessed on 25 August 2023.

21 @SriSri, X (formerly Twitter), 9 November 2019, 1.32 p.m. https://tinyurl.com/y76sfvjw. Accessed on 25 August 2023.

22 'Yoga Guru Ramdev on Ayodhya Verdict; Says SC Verdict Has Honoured All Sides', *Times Now News*, 9 November 2023, https://tinyurl.com/328rn8m9. Accessed on 25 August 2023.

23 @AvdheshanandG, X (formerly Twitter), 9 November 2019, 11.21 a.m. https://tinyurl.com/3tn4duca. Accessed on 25 August 2023.

24 'Ayodhya Dispute: Comparing the Legacy of Ram & Babur', *Isha Foundation*, https://tinyurl.com/27ubkhesr. Accessed on 25 August 2023.

25 Khurshid, Salman, 'Ayodhya Verdict Nudges Us to Look Back at How Much We Have Lost over Years of Conflict', *The Indian Express*, 11

November 2019, https://tinyurl.com/ru5vm549. Accessed on 25 August 2023.

26   Mehta, P.B., 'Ayodhya's Ram Temple Is First Real Colonisation of Hinduism by Political Power', *The Indian Express*, 5 August 2020, https://tinyurl.com/26ypv88y. Accessed on 25 August 2023.

27   Firdaus, Syed Ashraf, 'Muslims Ready to Give up Babri Claim, Their Leaders Are Not', *Rediff.com*, 23 Novemeber 2018, https://tinyurl.com/5n62dz8b. Accessed on 9 November 2023.

28   @RanaAyuub, X (formerly Twitter), 10 November 2019, 10.13 p.m., https://tinyurl.com/yktxd6k8. Accessed on 25 August 2023.

29   'Asaduddin Owaisi on Ayodhya Verdict: "Supreme but not infallible"', *The Indian Express*, 9 November 2019, https://tinyurl.com/4hjarxum. Accessed on 25 August 2023.

30   'Ayodhya Verdict: Zafaryab Jilani Says Sunni Waqf Board Not Satisfied with Judgment, May File a Review Petition', *CNBCTV18*, 9 November 2019, https://tinyurl.com/dmtvjxzk. Accessed on 25 August 2023.

31   Ahmed, S, 'No Blood Shed, Amicable Solution Best Part of Supreme Court Verdict: Muslims', *The Times of India*, 10 November 2019, https://tinyurl.com/29a7tysh. Accessed on 25 August 2023.

32   'Muslim Leaders, Intellectuals Meet; Say Ayodhya Verdict Should Be Respected by All, *India Today*, 25 March 2022, https://tinyurl.com/57rkx8vn. Accessed on 25 August 2023.

33   Bajpai, N, 'Ram Is of Everyone, He Is in Everyone: President Ram Nath Kovind', *The New Indian Express*, 29 August 2021, https://tinyurl.com/3b6n9myw, Accessed on 25 August 2023.

Chapter 4: From Verdict to Vision

1   @narendramodi, X (formerly Twitter), 5 February 2020, 12.10 p.m., https://tinyurl.com/535txrm6. Accessed on 14 November 2023.

2   Dixit, P., 'Ram Temple Trust: Ten Out of the 15 Members Named', *Hindustan Times*, 5 February 2020, https://tinyurl.com/ycxdyts9. Accessed on 1 September 2023.

3   'Ram Temple Trust: God's Advocate, Nirmohi Akhara, Dalit Gets on Board, Check Full List', *India Today*, 5 February 2020, https://tinyurl.com/muyy5e9k. Accessed on 1 September 2023.

4   Sharma, H., 'Ram Temple in Ayodhya: Parasaran First Trustee, 15-Member Trust Office Has His Home Address', *The Indian Express*, 6 February 2020, https://tinyurl.com/y6fwjdhr. Accessed on 1 September 2023.

5   Uprety, A., 'Who Is Mahant Nritya Gopal Das, Head of Ram Janmabhoomi Nyas', *The Week*, 6 November 2019, https://tinyurl.com/32p5ztu2. Accessed on 16 September 2023.

6   'PM Modi's Ex-principal Secy Nripendra Misra to Head Ram Temple Construction Panel', *The Indian Express*, 19 February 2020, https://tinyurl.com/bdjh3xsz. Accessed on 14 September 2023.

7   'Nripendra Misra, Modi's Trusted Former IAS Officer, Will Head Ram Temple Construction Panel', *The Print*, 19 February 2020, https://tinyurl.com/bdw4k5b7. Accessed on 12 September 2023.

8   '"Ram Temple as per Vhp Model but Grander", Says Mahant Nritya Gopal Das after Being Appointed Head of Mandir Trust,' *Swarajya Magazine*, 20 February 2020, https://tinyurl.com/r2rzxnjh. Accessed on 16 September 2023.

9   PTI, 'Ayodhya Ram Temple to Cost About ₹1,800 Crore: Trust', *The Hindu*, 11 September 2022, https://tinyurl.com/mryp4hbz. Accessed on 20 October 2023.

10   Pandey, N. 'VHP to Reach Out to PM Modi, President Seeking Contribution for Ram Mandir Construction', *The Print*, 16 December 2020, https://tinyurl.com/32kfx9hd. Accessed on 15 October 2023.

11   '"Shri Ram Mandir Nidhi Samarpan" Drive to Start from Jan 15', *India Post*, 17 December 2020, https://tinyurl.com/3hxjtndh. Accessed on 16 September 2023.

12   Khan, A.A., 'Ram Temple Coffers Brim with Rs 2,100 Crore on Last Day of Crowdfunding', *The Times of India*, 28 February 2021, https://tinyurl.com/34v8wf5d. Accessed on 16 November 2023.

13   Bajpai, Namita., 'Biggest Fund Raising Drive Launched to Collect Donations for Ram Temple Construction in Ayodhya,' *The New Indian Express*, 15 January 2021, https://tinyurl.com/yn9zmu6h. Accessed on 10 October 2023.

14   PTI, 'Former UP MLA Donates Over Rs 1 Crore for Ram Temple Construction', *NDTV*, 15 January 2021, https://tinyurl.com/mt7rewkn. Accessed on 1 September 2023.

15   Shah, Pankaj, 'President, Yogi Adityanath among 1st to Donate for

Ram Temple', *The Times of India*, 16 January 2021, https://tinyurl.com/yj7f47cn. Accessed on 1 September 2023.

16   Gupta, M.D. 'Spiritual Leader Morari Bapu Highest Donor as Ram Temple Trust Collects over Rs 100 Cr', *The Print*, 30 December 2020, https://tinyurl.com/3h3puufr. Accessed on 1 September 2023.

17   Sikarwar, Dharam., 'List of Celebrities Who Have Donated for Ayodhya Ram Temple, Check Out Who Donated How Much?', *The Youth*, 3 February 2021, https://tinyurl.com/4r6hdcz8. Accessed on 16 September 2023.

18   Bajpai, Namita, 'Ayodhya Ram Temple Donations Cross Rs 1,500 Crore: Trust', *The New Indian Express*, 14 February 2021, https://tinyurl.com/ykmchfsh. Accessed on 1 September 2023.

19   '5 NE States Gave over Rs. 7 Crore for Construction of Ram Mandir', *Nagaland Post*, 18 March 2021, https://tinyurl.com/mf7mnzpx, Accessed on 1 September 2023.

20   'Rajasthan Donated Most for Ram Mandir Construction, Says Champat Rai', *ANI News*, 7 March 2021, https://tinyurl.com/yfymxssv. Accessed on 1 September 2023.

21   'Today's Sabaris–Bhakti Is the Binding Factor behind Donations by These Senior Citizens to Ram Mandir Nidhi Samarpan', *Hindu Post*, 30 January 2021, https://tinyurl.com/bdz6jdm9. Accessed on 16 September 2023.

22   Ibid.

23   'Muslim Woman Raising Funds for Ram Temple in Ayodhya', *Deccan Chronicle*, 20 January 2021, https://tinyurl.com/yv2rem88. Accessed on 1 September 2023.

24   Srivastava, Piyush, 'Donations for Ayodhya Temple Touch Rs 5,500 Crore, Says Construction Trust', *The Telegraph*, 29 June 2022, https://tinyurl.com/y8nuexfr. Accessed on 1 September 2023.

25   'Shri Ram Mandir Nidhi Samarpan drive', *India Post*, 24 December 2020, https://tinyurl.com/mrxx48fh. Accessed on 16 September 2023.

26   'In Pics: Ancient Idols, Shiv Ling Found during Ram Mandir Site Excavation in Ayodhya', *India TV News*, 21 May 2020, https://tinyurl.com/4e3at755. Accessed on 16 September 2023.

27   Kumar, Ravinder, 'Bhoomi Pujan of Ram Temple in Ayodhya: List of Persons Who Will Attend Historic Ceremony on August 5', *Zee*

News, 29 January 2020, https://tinyurl.com/4hyuut3u. Accessed on 1 October 2023.

28 'PM Modi Lays Foundation for Ram Temple in Ayodhya', *Economic Times*, 5 August 2020, https://tinyurl.com/tv2y3hrj. Accessed on 1 October 2023.

29 Ibid.

30 Ibid.

31 'Ayodhya Ram Mandir Muhurat: Know What Is Abhijeet Muhurat and Why Has It Been Chosen for the Bhumi Pujan', *Times Now Digital*, 5 August 2020, https://tinyurl.com/2fjtd4hv . Accessed on 1 October 2023.

32 'Achary Ganeshvar Shastri Honge Jagadaguru Ramanandachary Puraskar Se Sammanit, Nikala Tha Raam Mandir Ke Shilanyas Ka Muhurt (Acharya Ganeshwar Shastri to Be Conferred with Jagadaguru Ramanandachary Prize, Had Calculated the Auspicious Time for Ram Mandir Foundation Laying Ceremony)', *TV9 Bharatvarsh*, 3 February 2021, https://tinyurl.com/4eydxrbb. Accessed on 15 October 2023.

33 Kaushika, Pragya, 'PM Modi Offered Silver Kalash at Bhoomi Pujan of Ram Temple, Wore "Kusha Ki Pavitri" in Place of Gold Ring', *ANI News*, 5 August 2020, https://tinyurl.com/8hhymxdr. Accessed on 15 October 2023.

34 ANI, '9 Bricks From Devotees, Water From 100 Rivers Used For Ram Temple Rituals', *NDTV*, 5 August 2020, https://tinyurl.com/4evbprju. Accessed on 10 October 2023.

35 Ibid.

36 Ibid.

37 IANS, 'Sangam Soil, Water for "Bhumi Pujan" of Ram Temple', *National Herald*, 22 July 2020, https://tinyurl.com/4zhkf3fk. Accessed on 10 October 2023.

38 ANI, '9 Bricks From Devotees, Water From 100 Rivers Used For Ram Temple Rituals', *NDTV*, 5 August 2020, https://tinyurl.com/4evbprju. Accessed on 10 October 2023.

39 'Ram Mandir Bhumi Pujan: Full text of PM Narendra Modi's speech in Ayodhya', *The Indian Express*, 5 August 2020, https://tinyurl.com/5n87rbff. Accessed on 14 October 2023.

40 Ibid.

41 Ibid.

42 PTI, 'Huge Digital Billboard of Ayodhya Ram Temple Shines in New York's Times Square', *Mint*, 5 August 2020, https://tinyurl.com/bdcmkx3u. Accessed on 10 October 2023.

43 'A Historical and Emotional Day: L.K. Advani Speaks On Ram Mandir Bhoomi Pujan', YouTube, https://tinyurl.com/32yctb7d. Accessed on 16 November 2023.

44 Khan, Fatima, '"Ram Is Love, Ram Is Justice"—Rahul Gandhi Breaks His Silence on Ram Mandir', *The Print*, 5 August 2020, https://tinyurl.com/2auakxtr. Accessed on 1 October 2023.

45 Dutta, Prabhash K., 'Ayodhya Ram Mandir Bhoomi Pujan: 5 Controversies Explained', *India Today*, 15 July 2021, https://tinyurl.com/mtpm2aak. Accessed on 1 September 2023.

46 Chishti, S., 'Explained: Story of 67 Acres in Ayodhya Adjoining Babri Site, Now with Ram Temple Trust', *The Indian Express*, 6 August 2020, https://tinyurl.com/rstwcjhk. Accessed on 8 September 2023.

47 Bajpai, N., 'Ayodhya Temple: Trust Buys Adjoining Land for Rs 1 Crore to Expand Ram Janmabhoomi Complex', *The New Indian Express*, 3 March 2021, https://tinyurl.com/yeykuu8k. Accessed on 16 September 2023.

48 PTI, 'Ram Mandir Trust Buys 1.15 Lakh Square of Land for Security Forces, Devotees', *The Print*, 20 March 2021, https://tinyurl.com/57ncpuf6. Accessed on 16 September 2023.

49 'Ram Mandir Trust Purchases 1.15 Lakh Sq Ft of Land in Ayodhya', *The Indian Express*, 20 March 2021, https://tinyurl.com/29uwarm3. Accessed on 6 September 2023.

50 Dixit, P. 'Trust Acquires More Land to Expand Ayodhya Temple Complex', *Hindustan Times*, 10 July 2021, https://tinyurl.com/4uxtxhw7. Accessed on 16 September 2023.

51 Bajpai, Namita, '280-Feet Wide, 300-Feet Long and 161-Feet Tall: Ayodhya Ram Temple Complex to Be World's Third-Largest" *The New Indian Express*, 5 August 2020, https://tinyurl.com/ypm5ueyk. Accessed on 6 September 2023.

52 'Champat Rai on Ram Temple Trust Land Purchase Controversy| Ram Mandir Scam | Ram Mandir Land Scam', YouTube, https://tinyurl.com/8hh49ebm. Accessed on 6 September 2023.

53 'Nagara Architecture Of Ayodhya's Magnificent Ram Mandir Explained With Pictures', *Swarajyamag*, 5 August 2020, https://tinyurl.com/24f9uxck. Accessed on 6 September 2023.

54 Vij-Aurora, Bhavana, 'The Man Who Measured Land With His Feet Awaits Construction Of Ram Mandir In Ayodhya He Designed', *Outlook India*, 5 August 2020, https://tinyurl.com/5se54rx7. Accessed on 6 September 2023.

55 Ibid.

56 Misra, Leena, 'Meet the Sompuras, Master Architects Who are Building the Ram Temple in Ayodhya', *The Indian Express*, 6 August 2020, https://tinyurl.com/2dx8jn5t. Accessed on 6 September 2023.

57 Bajpai, Namita., '280-Feet Wide, 300-Feet Long and 161-Feet Tall: Ayodhya Ram Temple Complex to Be World's Third-Largest', *The New Indian Express*, 4 August 2020, https://tinyurl.com/ypm5ueyk. Accessed on 6 September 2023.

58 'Shri Ram Mandir Ayodhya', *Temples Vibhaga*, https://tinyurl.com/mr323hk7. Accessed on 6 September 2023.

59 Ibid.

60 @ShriRamTeerth, X (formerly Twitter), 4 August 2020, 2.40 p.m. https://tinyurl.com/yv92kh48. Accessed on 6 September 2023.

61 Mishra, Sunita. 'Everything You Need to Know About Ayodhya Ram Mandir,' *Housing News*, 10 November 2023, https://tinyurl.com/5n7bvthd. Accessed on 16 September 2023.

62 'Ayodhya: Ram Temple's Ground Floor in Final Construction Phase', *Mint*, 13 June 2023, https://tinyurl.com/3msraj2m. Accessed on 16 September 2023.

63 'Nagara Architecture Of Ayodhya's Magnificent Ram Mandir Explained With Pictures', *Swarajyamag*, 5 August 2020, https://tinyurl.com/24f9uxck. Accessed on 6 September 2023.

64 'Ayodhya: Ram Temple's Ground Floor in Final Construction Phase', *Mint*, 13 June 2023, https://tinyurl.com/3msraj2m. Accessed on 16 September 2023.

65 Khan, Arshad Afzaal, 'Ayodhya's Ram Mandir Will Not Need Repairs for Thousand Years', *India Times*, 18 July 2023, https://tinyurl.com/bdatze4p. Accessed on 16 September 2023.

66 'Ayodhya: Ram Temple's Ground Floor in Final Construction Phase', *Mint*, 13 June 2023, https://tinyurl.com/3msraj2m. Accessed on 16

November 2023.

67 'Marbles from Rajasthan, Gold Door: What the Ram Temple in Ayodhya Will Look Like', *Firstpost*, 13 July 2023, https://tinyurl.com/4p9vujrh. Accessed on 16 November 2023.

68 Khan, Arshad Afzaal, 'Ram Temple in Ayodhya to Open for Public by January 2024', *India Times*, 26 October 2022, https://tinyurl.com/bdfd7p5b. Accessed on 16 November 2023.

69 ANI, 'Three Sculptors Engaged in Making Lord Ram's Idol: Ayodhya Temple Trust', *The Economic Times,* 31 May 2023, https://tinyurl.com/4xmv8z93. Accessed on 16 November 2023.

70 Pandey, Kirti, 'PM Modi To Carry Ram Lalla Idol From Makeshift Temple To New Ayodhya Mandir?: Reports', *Times Now*, 11 November 2023, https://tinyurl.com/yc8xs5nt. Accessed on 16 November 2023.

71 Singh, A., 'Ram Mandir Pran Pratishtha on January 22', *Jagran English*, 26 September 2023, https://tinyurl.com/7k89yxkj. Accessed on 28 September 2023.

72 PTI, 'Ram Mandir Trust Invites Designing Ideas from Professionals', *Deccan Herald*, 5 November 2020, https://tinyurl.com/y3f233kw. Accessed on 28 October 2023.

73 Mishra, Avaneesh, 'Ram Temple in Ayodhya: Experts' Panel to Review All, from Design to Construction', *Indian Express*, 15 December 2020, https://tinyurl.com/yp3tu7ps. Accessed on 6 September 2023.

74 IANS, 'L&T to Oversee the Construction of Ram Temple: Vishwa Hindu Parishad', *Business Standard*, 3 March 2020, https://tinyurl.com/44wddn55. Accessed on 6 September 2023.

75 Khan, A.A., 'Ram Temple to Be Quake-Resistant with 1,000-Year Life Span', *India Times*, 8 August 2020, https://tinyurl.com/3b4vcrjf. Accessed on 28 October 2023.

76 IANS, 'Ram Temple in Ayodhya Will Last One Thousand Years: Champat Rai', *Bhaskar Live*, 18 July 2023, https://tinyurl.com/yd2jm92z. Accessed on 28 October 2023.

77 @ShriRamTeerth, X (formerly Twitter), 20 May 2020, 7.30 p.m. https://tinyurl.com/5yv9je7n. Accessed on 16 September 2023.

78 Pandey, Vishal, 'Only 175 Guests Invited for Bhoomi Pujan Ceremony of Ram Temple on August 5', *Zee News*, 4 August 2020, https://tinyurl.com/55s5cnxe. Accessed on 16 November 2023.

79 'Temple Construction Hits Loose Sand Hurdle', *The Indian Express*,

6 December 2020, https://tinyurl.com/spmecw3r. Accessed on 16 September 2023.

80 @ShriRamTeerth, X (formerly Twitter), 4 September 2020, 10.11 p.m., https://tinyurl.com/y54hc8ff. Accessed on 16 November 2023.

81 'Carved Stones Being Moved from Workshop to the Ram Temple Premises', YouTube, https://tinyurl.com/2ey2vk7h. Accessed on 16 November 2023.

82 PTI, 'Eight-Member Expert Panel Set Up to Supervise Ram Temple Foundation-Laying Work', *The New India Express*, 13 December 2020, https://tinyurl.com/593u6rtx. Accessed on 16 November 2023; '12 Dec, 2020', *Shri Ram Janmbhoomi Teerth Kshetra*, 21 April 2021, https://tinyurl.com/y6uks3m3. Accessed on 16 November 2023.

83 '29 Dec, 2020: Highlights of the Meeting of Construction Committee', *Shri Ram Janmbhoomi Teerth Kshetra*, 21 April 2021, https://tinyurl.com/4aa82zk5. Accessed on 16 November 2023.

84 '6 Feb 2021', *Shri Ram Janmbhoomi Teerth Kshetra*, 21 April 2021, https://tinyurl.com/56n37awm. Accessed on 16 November 2023.

85 Khan, Arshad Afzaal, 'Uttar Pradesh: 9 Shilas Worshipped by PM Narendra Modi at 'Garb Griha', *The Times of India*, 18 May 2021, https://tinyurl.com/y6e5ubhv. Accessed on 16 November 2023.

86 Ray, Meenakshi, 'Ram Mandir Foundation Complete; Granite from Karnataka, Mirzapur's Sandstone to Be Used Next', *Hindustan Times*, 17 September 2021, https://tinyurl.com/287xfdek. Accessed on 16 November 2023.

87 'Shriram Janmabhoomi Temple 3D Walk Through | Mandir Banane Ke Baad Kaisa Dikhega (How Will the Temple Look Once Made)', YouTube, https://tinyurl.com/8d6ry9hn. Accessed on 16 November 2023.

88 PTI, 'Rajasthan's Carved Stone Slabs Reach Ayodhya For Ram Temple Construction', *NDTV*, 5 April 2022, https://tinyurl.com/a6muyayn. Accessed on 16 November 2023.

89 'PM Performs Darshan and Pooja of Bhagwan Shree Ramlala Virajman in Ayodhya, Uttar Pradesh', *PMIndia*, 23 October 2022, https://tinyurl.com/2u8pph6e. Accessed on 16 November 2023.

90 'Ayodhya Ram Temple: Construction Underway for Sanctum Sanctorum | Pics', *Mint*, 25 November 2022, https://tinyurl.com/ywxmtk6n. Accessed on 16 November 2023.

91 'Ayodhya Ram Temple to Have Gold-Plated Doors in Sanctum Sanctorum, a Golden Throne for Ram Lalla', *Zee News*, 10 November 2023, https://tinyurl.com/4ubpwpca. Accessed on 16 November 2023.

92 PTI, 'Ram Temple's Sanctum Sanctorum Ready, Idol Consecration between Jan 16-24: Trust General Secy', *The Print*, 20 August 2023, https://tinyurl.com/ye2x2sap. Accessed on 16 September 2023.

93 'Ayodhya's Ram Temple Set to Enthrall Visitors with 600Kg Narmadeshwar Mahadev Shivling', *The Times of India*, 24 August 2023, https://tinyurl.com/ysuw3c4j. Accessed on 16 September 2023; 'Grand Temple Will Be Built for Ram Lalla Who Lived in Temporary Tent for Years, Says PM Modi', *The Hindu*, 20 August 2020, https://tinyurl.com/373scr5e. Accessed on 01 September 2023.

94 Verma, S., 'Foreign Devotees Allowed to Fund Ram Temple Construction As MHA Approves FCRA | Details', *News18*, 18 October 2023, https://tinyurl.com/4ktm7re7. Accessed on 1 September 2023.

95 @narendramodi, X (formerly Twitter), 24 October 2023, 9.31 p.m., https://tinyurl.com/bdfh3e45. Accessed on 01 September 2023.

96 @ShriRamTeerth, X (formerly Twitter), 25 October 2023, 7.57 p.m., https://tinyurl.com/3rhwa6u3. Accessed on 01 September 2023.

97 @narendramodi, X (formerly Twitter), 25 October 2023, 7.46 p.m., https://tinyurl.com/3shypauk. Accessed on 16 November 2023.

98 @ShriRamTeerth, X (formerly Twitter), 3 November 2023, 5.26 p.m., https://tinyurl.com/bds4ahbk. Accessed on 16 November 2023.

99 @ShriRamTeerth, X (formerly Twitter), 12 November 2023, 12.37 a.m., https://tinyurl.com/2bzv3ytf. Accessed on 16 November 2023.

100 'Ayodhya "Deepotsav" Sets New Guinness World Record with over 22.23 Lakh Diyas', *The Times of* india, 12 November 2023, https://tinyurl.com/mryvuz4j. Accessed on 16 November 2023.

101 '"After 500 Yrs of Sacrifices, Shri Ram Going To...": Up CM as Ayodhya Mandir Illuminated for Diwali — Watch', *ABP News,* 12 November 2023, https://tinyurl.com/mt5csfd8. Accessed on 16 November 2023.

102 @ANI, X (formerly Twitter), 13 November 2023, 4.21 p.m. https://tinyurl.com/2dm4vskh. Accessed on 16 November 2023.

103 Sen, Shilpi, 'Ayodhya Mein Ram Lalla Ki Pran Pratishtha Se Pehle VHP Nikalega "Shaurya Yatra", Janein Kya Hai Yojana (In Ayodhya, VHP Will Take Out A Valour Procession Prior to Ram

Lalla's Consecration Ceremony, Know the Programme)', *UP Tak*, 30 September 2023, https://tinyurl.com/24h62ex7. Accessed on 16 November 2023.

104 Shalabh, 'PM Narendra Modi Likely to Carry Ram Lalla Idol from Makeshift to New Ayodhya Temple', *The Times of India*, 3 November 2023, https://tinyurl.com/jhkhbujr. Accessed on 16 November 2023.

105 'Historic! PM Narendra Modi May Break Protocol, Walk 500 Metres to Carry Ram Lalla Idol to New Ayodhya Temple - What We Know So Far ', *ET Now*, 5 November 2023, https://tinyurl.com/4kmbs7es. Accessed on 16 November 2023.

106 '"Ram Mandir...": Two Things PM Modi Told His Ex-Aide Nripendra Misra On Ayodhya Temple', YouTube, https://tinyurl.com/54w3z8e3. Accessed on 28 October 2023.

Chapter 5: Echoes of Treta in Ayodhya: Ancient Legacy, Modern Transformation

1 'Ayodhya, Uttar Pradesh, India', *Latlog.net*, https://tinyurl.com/y9m4u236. Accessed on 22 November 2023.

2 ANI, 'UP Govt to Build Ramayana, Mahabharata Circuits under New Tourism Policy', *The Print*, 16 November 2022, https://tinyurl.com/4pe7aaxw. Accessed on 25 September 2023.

3 Sinha, Saurabh, 'Taj Group To Open Three Hotels In Ayodhya, 2 To Be Ready By 2027', *The Times of India*, 22 April 2023, https://tinyurl.com/3u775tz7. Accessed on 16 September 2023.

4 A UP government document dated 12 April 2018 stated: 'The international tourist market is largely untapped in the case of Ayodhya. The number of international tourists visiting Ayodhya has been very low, i.e. approx. 24,000 in the year 2017. Ayodhya does not carry a significant spiritual brand such as Haridwar or Varanasi, which have a brand perception of being able to "wash away sins" (Haridwar), or attain spiritual freedom (Varanasi). It does not offer the brand equity of being a "spiritual destination" or be part of a "backpacker's trail"—either of which has been instrumental in tapping into the international tourist market.'

5 Singh, P.V., 'Exponential Rise! Property Rates In Ayodhya Double After Ram Temple Bhoomi Pujan - Check Factors Leading To Real Estate Boom', *Zee Business*, 28 September 2020, https://tinyurl.com/

bdf9kdn4. Accessed on 17 September 2023.

6   Rawat, V. S., 'Uttar Pradesh Govt Set To Launch 'New Ayodhya'
     Project In The Next 2 Months', *Business Standard,* https://tinyurl.
     com/ye2r5z27. Accessed on 16 September 2023.

7   IANS, '"New Ayodhya" to rise by 2024', *Dtnext,* 23 October 2022,
     https://tinyurl.com/apdutfnz. Accessed on 16 September 2023.

8   TNN, 'Up Chief Minister Yogi Adityanath Inaugurates Projects Worth
     Rs 212 Crore In Ayodhya', *The Times of India,* 16 June 2023, https://
     tinyurl.com/4j3hc37u. Accessed on 16 September 2023.

9   'UP Cabinet approves proposal for world-class bust station at
     Ayodhya', *India Today,* 14 June 2021, https://tinyurl.com/8unr767f.
     Accessed on 1 November 2023.

10   'Grand Ram Mandir: How A Massive Infrastructure Push by Modi
     and Yogi is Set to Transform Ayodhya', *Swaraj Magazine,* 9 November
     2022, https://tinyurl.com/mrxyan44. Accessed on 1 November 2023.

11   Ibid.

12   'Religious Tourism in UP: Naimisharanya to Be Developed on Lines
     Of Ayodhya and Kashi', *Hindustan Times,* 11 July 2022, https://
     tinyurl.com/5n7facs7. Accessed on 16 September 2023.

13   'Ramayana Era Tree Cover for Mandir Campus', *The Times of India,*
     14 December 2020, https://tinyurl.com/3tb8rkvc. Accessed on 16
     September 2023.

14   Khan, A.A., 'Navya Ayodhya Soon Near "Ram's Abode" to Provide
     Moksha', *The Times of India,* 1 August 2018, https://tinyurl.com/
     yt57cuxc. Accessed on 16 September 2023.

15   Ibid.

16   'In Big Ayodhya Revamp, Yogi Adityanath Plans a World-Class
     Township Based on London', *The Economic Times,* 1 August 2018,
     https://tinyurl.com/3r84un4c. Accessed on 16 November 2023.

17   Srivastava, R. 'In Navya Ayodhya, See 7d Ramlila, Ramayana Light
     and Sound Show, *The Times of India,* 17 October 2017, https://tinyurl.
     com/rvpx29tx. Accessed on 16 October 2023.

18   TNN, 'Gujarat Govt to Help Build Ayodhya Ram Statue', *The Times
     of India,* 3 March 2019, https://tinyurl.com/4x7p4se8. Accessed on
     16 October 2023.

19   'Ayodhya's Luxury Cruise Service "Jatayu" to Commence on
     September 8', *Moneycontrol,* 7 September 2023, https://tinyurl.

com/5n83pfwv. Accessed on 16 September 2023.

20 'Welcome to Ram Land! What Is the Disneyland-like Theme Park Coming to Ayodhya?', *Firstpost,* 10 May 2023, https://tinyurl. com/2s3mu94c. Accessed on 27 October 2023.

21 Ibid.

22 PTI, 'Ayodhya to Get 'Temple Museum' Soon: Up Govt', *Deccan Herald*, 2 September 2023, https://tinyurl.com/dpjz8uzv. Accessed on 16 September 2023.

23 Samvad News Agency, 'Guptar Ghat Ke Paas 75 Acre Mein Banega Sriram Chalit Manas Anubhav Kendra (Sriram Chalit Manas Anubhav Kendra to Be Built Next to Guptar Ghat in 75 Acres)', *Amar Ujala*, 23 September 2023, https://tinyurl.com/2sts5eme. Accessed on 27 October 2023.

24 Ibid.

25 'Lotus-Shaped Fountain Worth Rs 100 Crore to Come Up near Ram Temple in Ayodhya', *India Today*, 25 September 2023, https://tinyurl. com/5h27ydmt. Accessed on 27 October 2023.

26 Ibid.

27 Khan, A. A., 'Roof-Top Cafes in Ayodhya for Majestic View of Ram Temple', *The Times of India*, 2 August 2023, https://tinyurl.com/ msenkv4h. Accessed on 16 September 2023.

28 IANS, 'Ayodhya to Have 25 Ram Stambhs on 17 Km Road to Ram Temple', *The Statesman*, 16 July 2023, https://tinyurl.com/y2zvu4ux. Accessed on 16 September 2023.

29 Dixit, Pawan, 'Ram Temple Work in Full Swing, Completion Nears', *Hindustan Times,* 9 July 2023, https://tinyurl.com/3fu9mmu3. Accessed on 17 September 2023.

30 '25 Ram Stambhs to Come Up on 17-Km Road to Ram Temple in Ayodhya', *Hindustan Times*, 18 July 2023, https://tinyurl. com/3r9bx89r. Accessed on 17 September 2023.

31 'Ayodhya Haat to Be Another Attraction in Temple Town', *Hindustan Times*, 17 August 2023, https://tinyurl.com/s4kanvbn. Accessed on 17 September 2023.

32 'Ayodhya Nagri Mein Char Chand Laga Dega Sarayu nadi Ke Tat Par Banane Wala "Haat" ('Haat' to Be Built on the Banks of Saryu River Will Add Charm to Ayodhya City)', *Khas Khabar*, 18 August 2023, https://tinyurl.com/45zmw7ur. Accessed on 17 September 2023.

33   Saxena, A, 'Transforming Ayodhya: Government Announces Global Competition To Showcase Cultural Heritage Through Artworks In The Temple Town', *Swarajyamag*, https://tinyurl.com/yrxdfbsa. Accessed on 17 September 2023.

34   'Global Design Competition for Theme-based design work on life of Lord Shri Ram', *Ayodhya Development Authority*, http://ayodhyacontest.com/contest/contest. Accessed on 17 September 2023.

35   '16 Places to Visit in Ayodhya', *Holidify.com*, https://tinyurl.com/wreezcy9. Accessed on 17 September 2023.

36   *Incredible India*, https://tinyurl.com/4258zrde. Accessed on 17 September 2023.

37   'Significance of Panchavati for Shri Rama Devotees', *Times Now Digital*, 30 July 2020, https://tinyurl.com/3y3fp9s6. Accessed on 28 September 2023.

38   Goel, Anuradha, 'Ramtek – The Ramayana Footprint in Vidharbha', *India Tales*, 9 February 2023, https://tinyurl.com/ymxy3p55. Accessed on 17 September 2023.

39   Ibid.

40   'Turturiya', *Ram Van Gaman Path*, https://tinyurl.com/nnwj22pp. Accessed on 17 September 2023.

41   'Janakpur', *Mount Mania,* https://tinyurl.com/yz3bzcfc. Accessed on 17 September 2023.